World War One

A Very Peculiar History™

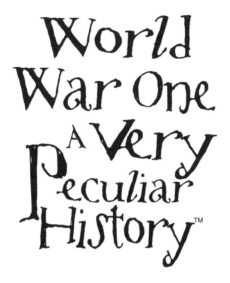

'The lamps are going out all over
Europe. We shall not see them lit again
in our lifetime.'

Sir Edward Grey, British Foreign Secretary,
3 August 1914, after war was declared

For Baha (my grandfather Jack
Sanders), one of millions whose life
was forever changed by the war.
JP

Editors: Victoria England, Jamie Pitman
Editorial assistants: Rob Walker, Mark Williams
Illustrations: David Antram, Mark Bergin,
Mark Peppé, Gerald Wood

Published in Great Britain in MMXII by
Book House, an imprint of
The Salariya Book Company Ltd
25 Marlborough Place, Brighton BN1 1UB
www.salariya.com
www.book-house.co.uk

HB ISBN-13: 978-1-908177-00-1

1 3 5 7 9 8 6 4 2

A CIP catalogue record for this book is available
from the British Library.

Printed and bound in Dubai.

Printed on paper from sustainable sources.

Visit our website at **www.book-house.co.uk**
or go to **www.salariya.com**
for **free** electronic versions of:
You Wouldn't Want to be an Egyptian Mummy!
You Wouldn't Want to be a Roman Gladiator!
You Wouldn't Want to be a Polar Explorer!
**You Wouldn't Want to sail on a 19th-Century
Whaling Ship!**

World War One
A Very Peculiar History™

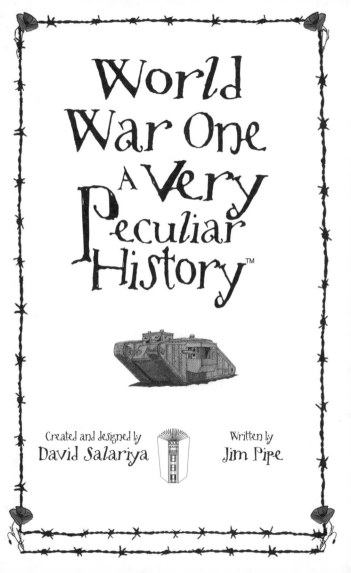

Created and designed by
David Salariya

Written by
Jim Pipe

'I adore war. It's like a big picnic without the objectlessness of a picnic. I've never been so well or happy. No one grumbles at one for being dirty.'

British officer Julian Grenfell, professional soldier and poet

'A short time ago, death was the cruel stranger, the visitor with the flannel footsteps...today it is the mad dog in the house.'

Georges Duhamel, French novelist and doctor at Verdun

'It takes 15,000 casualties to train a major-general.'

General Foch

'We were not making war against Germany, we were being ordered about in the King's war with Germany.'

English novelist H. G. Wells, 1914

'All along the line, Englishmen could be seen throwing their arms in the air and collapsing, never to move again.'

A German soldier describes the Somme attack

Contents

The war at a glance

It can be hard to get your head around the enormity of the Great War. A few facts and figures to get you started:

- **3.2 kph** was the average speed of attacking British troops in the First Battle of the Somme. Tanks weren't much quicker, a dawdling 7 kph.

- **11 per cent** of France's entire population were killed or wounded in the Great War.

- **23 days** was the time a typical Royal Flying Corps (British) pilot could expect to survive in 1917 once he'd arrived on the Western Front. Pilots who weren't killed, wounded, or taken prisoner were often posted to the reserves due to 'nerves' (mental breakdown).

- **51 kg** was the minimum weight required to join the British Army.

- **58 per cent** of British troops were wounded by shells, compared with 40 per cent killed by rifle or machine gun fire, with just 1 per cent killed by bayonets.

- **74 metres** was the average advance made by the British army during the Third Battle of Ypres in the six months from June to December 1917 (that's less than 0.5 m a day).

- **60 seconds** was the time a 6-inch (150 mm) howitzer shell usually spent in the air before hitting its target. However, the sound arrived in about 1.5 seconds, so experienced soldiers in the trenches had time to work out if it was heading their way.

- **65 per cent** of Australians serving in the war were killed or wounded, the highest proportion among any nation.

- **230 combatants** on average died every single hour, throughout the war.

- **263 tonnes** was the weight of the Schneider 520 mm howitzer, the biggest gun of the Great War. Its gun carriage was over 30 metres long and it could hurl a 1,400 kg shell over 16 kilometres.

- **1,500 letters** were written by General Hindenburg to his wife Gertrude during the course of the war.

- **1,510 kg** was the weight of the war's heaviest shell, delivered by an 18-inch (460-mm) gun mounted on HMS *General Wolfe*, a battleship known as a monitor built for attacking the shore. This ship fired 52 such shells at a railway bridge south of Ostend at a range of some 33 kilometres, which were also the longest shots of the war. Apparently most landed close to the target.

- **2,000 scientists** worked on the Germans' poison gas programme. Eight had won or went on to win the Nobel Prize (not for peace, it should be added).

- **10,000 church bells** from the German state of Prussia were melted down to make weapons.

- **12,000 bullets** were fired by a single machine gun at the Battle of Loos in 1915.

- **15,000 horseshoes** were worn out in the first few days of the war by French cavalry riding to Belgium on metalled roads.

- **600,000 Poles** were shipped to Germany to work on farms and factories, along with around 120,000 Belgians.

- **180,000 letters** written home by soldiers were read each week by French intelligence.

- **250,000 buildings** were destroyed in France during the war, including 1,500 schools.

- **423,000 kg** was the combined weight of the high explosive used in 19 giant mines on the Messines ridge shortly before the Third Battle of Ypres (with around 1/32nd of the power of the first atomic bomb dropped by the United States on the Japanese city of Hiroshima in 1945).

- **499 strikes** were held in Germany before the end of the war.

- **453,716 tonnes** was the amount of shipping sunk by the war's most successful U-boat (submarine) captain, Lothar de la Perière, during 14 voyages with the U-35. In total, he sank 194 merchant vessels and two gunboats.

- **27 million people** were killed by the Spanish flu epidemic.

- **32 million shells** were fired by the Germans and French during the Battle of Verdun in 1916. In places 10 shells fell on every square centimetre. When the war ended, the whole battlefield was planted with conifers. Walk among the trees today, and you'll still see the ground pockmarked with shell-holes.

- **140 million socks** were delivered to British troops, along with 50 million boots and some 10 million cardigans. Don't laugh, these were essential items in the trenches.

- **4,000 planes** were lost by Britain during the war, the highest figure for any nation.

Sopwith Camel 1918

'What a bloodbath...
Hell cannot be this dreadful.'

Albert Joubaire, French soldier at Verdun, 1916

'You were between the devil and the deep blue sea. If you go forward, you'll likely be shot, if you go back you'll be court-martialled and shot, so what the hell do you do? What can you do? You just go forward because that's the only bloke you can take your knife in, that's the bloke you are facing.'

Private W. Hay

'I just crawled on my hands and knees and got back in the trench... We got annihilated. There was nobody left.'

A British infantryman describes the slaughter on the Western Front

'Attaque à l'outrance!' (All-out attack!)

The philosophy of the École Supérieure de Guerre (French War College) before the war

INTRODUCTION

The Great War

Not for nothing is the First World War known as the Great War. Not because it was fun, though for many it certainly started out as an exciting adventure. Quite simply, it was a whopper, the biggest slugging match in world history. Some 65 million men from all four corners of the globe packed their kit and marched off to war, from teenagers to grandfathers in their sixties.

The fighting kicked off in Europe, but the rest of the world soon got dragged in, kicking and screaming, including some 2 million Africans. Another 3 million from the far-flung British

Empire answered the call to arms, shipped from Canada, Australia, New Zealand, South Africa and India. And, for the first time, the United States got its hands dirty in Europe. In all, 28 countries were involved, making this the first truly global war. Even Japan hopped on the bandwagon, hoping to grab German islands in the Pacific when no-one was looking,[1] while the Thais sneakily snatched twelve German ships when their king, Rama VI, boldy declared war on Germany in July 1917.[2]

For most people, the Great War conjures up images of muddy French trenches and young men being ripped to pieces by machine guns and almighty explosions. But as you'll see, there was a lot more to it than that – colossal battleships blazing at each other off the coast of South America, gunboats being lugged through the African rainforest, Italian and Austrian troops freezing to death in the Alps, and Lawrence of Arabia racing across the desert on his camel.

1. *It was a clever move. After a successful raid on the German base at Tsingtao on China's east coast, the Japanese troops were home by Christmas and only lost some 400 soldiers.*
2. *To be fair, Thailand also sent some 1,300 volunteers to the Western Front, including a number of pilots.*

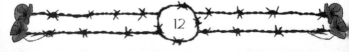

This was also the age of 'Total War': everyone took part. Ordinary citizens in their millions rolled up their sleeves to arm, clothe and feed their boys in the field. Factories churned out weapons and munitions, while ten thousand locomotives puffed and clattered as they shunted the troops to the front lines. And, for the first time, women and children on both sides became targets as bombs whistled down on homes and schools. In total, some 7 million civilians died in the conflict, including 500,000 Armenians massacred by Turkish forces.

Take your pick

A year after the war ended, a journalist writing for the London *Times* coined the phrase 'First World War'. You can also take your pick from:

- World War One
- The Great War
- The War of the Nations
- The War to End All Wars
- The War to Make the World Safe for Democracy (not quite so catchy!).

Despite the carnage, no-one knew when to stop. In 1871, the previous big European bunfight, it had taken the Germans just five months to defeat the French armies in the field. The Great War lasted for four years, from 1914 to 1918, and nearly 10 million soldiers died in the slaughter. Never before had a war been fought on so many battlefields and with such devastating weapons: machine guns, heavy artillery, gas, planes, tanks and submarines. Another 21 million combatants were wounded, many so badly they were never able to lead normal lives again. There were few families in Europe that did not lose a father or a son.[3]

The horror didn't end there. My great-grandfather James J. Sanders joined the Canadian Army[4] and fought on the Western Front. After surviving the war, he was awaiting orders in Liverpool when the Spanish flu hit. His regiment was billeted in a cinema. The disease spread like wildfire and

3. Though a whole generation was not lost, as is sometimes claimed –
by the mid-1920s the population in most European countries was back
to prewar levels.
4. The first time Canadian forces fought as a distinct unit, and in 1917,
under a Canadian-born commander, General Sir Arthur W. Currie.

within days everyone inside was struck down by the disease, apart from one man supposedly spared by being drunk on whisky.[5] It was a common story as the influenza epidemic swept through Asia into Europe and America. It killed more people than the Great War itself.

When you consider how millions died on the Western Front for gains of a few kilometres one way or the other, it's easy to wonder what on earth all the suffering was for. Yet back then many people believed they were fighting for a very good reason (to begin with, anyway). The Germans wanted to shake things up, to change the old world order. The British and Austrians liked things just the way they were, thank you very much. The French and Belgians fought most of the war on home turf – so for them it was a battle for freedom. Meanwhile Muslim Turkey, which entered on the side of Germany, declared a holy war on Britain, France and Russia.[6]

5. *The loss of a father was a huge blow in more ways than one – grieving families often faced financial ruin in the days before welfare payments. My grandfather Jack, the eldest son, had to leave school at 14 and get a job in a bank (which he hated) to help feed and clothe his brothers and sisters.*
6. *Overlooking the fact that many of the Muslims in the Ottoman empire saw their rulers, the Turks, as the enemy.*

10 Great War firsts

1. **First war to be fought on three continents:** Asia, Europe and Africa.

2. **First aerial bombers.** On 6 August 1914, a German Zeppelin bombed the Belgian city of Liège. A few weeks later, on 30 August 1914, a single plane dropped three bombs on Paris.

3. **First use of X-rays in war.** Scientist Marie Curie persuaded the French government that X-rays could save soldiers' lives by helping doctors to locate bullets, shrapnel and broken bones. By late October 1914, the first of 20 radiology vehicles (nicknamed 'petites Curies') were equipped and sent into service.

4. **First use of poison gas.** On 31 January 1915, 18,000 artillery shells loaded with tear gas were fired on Russian positions during the Battle of Bolimov. It was so cold that the chemicals froze and failed to work. Choking chlorine gas was first used at Ypres on 22 April 1915, against French Colonial troops from Martinique.

5. **First use of IQ tests.** Psychologist Robert Yerkes developed two tests that were used on over a million US recruits to judge who would make the best officers (though the tests were little better than a 1900s version of *Trivial Pursuit*, with questions on popular adverts and history).

6. **First use of the flamethrower.** This could throw out flames 20 metres long. Adopted by the German army in 1906, the flamethrower got its first serious workout on 30 July 1915, against British trenches at Hooge, during the Second Battle of Ypres. Though few enemy soldiers died of burns, the terrifying weapon flushed them out into the open where they were soon gunned down.

7. **First tanks used in battle.** Thirty-two British Mk I tanks were used at the Battle of the Somme on 15 September 1916. Just nine made it across no man's land to the German lines.

8. **First blood bank.** After US scientists discovered a way to store blood without it clotting, a 'blood depot' was set up by Oswald Hope Robertson, a US Army officer, while serving in France in 1917.

9. **First use of guide dogs by blinded soldiers.** A training programme was set up in Potsdam, Germany which trained German Shepherds (see page 24) as guide dogs for blind war veterans.

10. **First US President to visit Europe while in office.** Woodrow Wilson came to France in 1918 and spent six months in Paris preparing for the peace treaty at Versailles.

Whatever the intentions, the war certainly left its mark. Europe was left in tatters and the empires of Germany, Austria-Hungary, Turkey and Russia were left behind in the rubble. The war also kickstarted a revolution in Russia that kept the rest of the world on its toes for another seventy-odd years. In the UK, as in Germany, Britain, Canada and the United States, women finally got to vote. There was even the odd invention that didn't kill people, like the vacuum tubes that opened up a new world of popular radio in the 1920s.

In 1914 Fritz Haber, the German scientist who discovered how to make ammonia, advised the German government how to make explosives. He helped to organise gas attacks, as well as defences against them.

'**I**n Flanders fields
the poppies blow
Between the crosses,
row on row...'

One of the most moving poems of World War I
was written by John McCrae (1872–1918), a
Canadian army doctor of Scottish heritage.

Invention of the bomber plane in 1910

Bombs away!

'Fight on and fly on to the last drop of blood and the last drop of fuel, to the last beat of the heart.' The Red Baron

CHAPTER ONE

FIGHTING TALK

After years of careful planning, the Great War happened almost by accident. On the surface, things were looking up in 1914. In the previous 50 years, European countries had learned to work together, setting up the International Red Cross in 1863 and an international postal union 12 years later. Meanwhile, wonderful inventions like the telegraph, radio, motor car and plane were bringing people together. In February 1914, even the old enemies France and Germany shook hands in a trade deal with Turkey.[1] It was all thoroughly civilised. So why were the same countries trying to wipe each other out just a few months later?

1. Meanwhile, Britain and Germany remained good trading partners.

War plans

For over 30 years, the major nations of Europe busied themselves with plans for war:

France: Plan 17
Aim: To recapture Alsace and Lorraine (two neighbouring regions lost in 1871).
Tactic: Attack! Attack! Attack!
The Theory: The French soldiers can't lose, thanks to their natural fighting spirit.
The Reality: However brave you are, charging at well-trained troops that are dug in and armed with machine guns is a recipe for disaster.

Germany: Schlieffen Plan
Aim: To deliver a swift knockout blow to France before Russia gets her armies into the field.
Tactic: Invade through Belgium (it's very flat).
The Theory: If everything goes to schedule, we'll be sipping coffee in Paris within 40 days.
The Reality: Very nearly worked. But as the German army sped towards Paris, it got stretched too thin, allowing the French to counter-attack.

Austria-Hungary: Plans B and R
Aim: To crush Serbia into submission.
Tactic: Plan B – Attack Serbia, while defending against possible Russian invasion. Plan R allows more troops to defend against Russia.
The Theory: Germany will help out in the north.

The Reality: The Germans sent the bulk of their troops west, so Austria was left to fight Russia alone and got badly mauled.

Russia: Plans G and A (also known as 19)
Aim: To defeat Germany by soaking up the initial attack then grinding the enemy down.
Tactic: Russia is just too big to conquer – even Napoleon failed miserably back in 1812.
The Theory: Plan G expects a full-scale German attack on Russia, while the later Plan A correctly predicts a German attack on France first.
The Reality: Plan A was launched. The attack on Eastern Germany ended in a crushing defeat for Russia at the Battle of Tannenberg.

Britain: None
Aim: Defend the Empire
Tactic: Rule the Waves!
The Theory: Don't get drawn into a European war.
The Reality: OK chaps, we probably should come to the Belgians' rescue. It is the decent thing to do, after all.

This armed French airship was used by the British to protect the English Channel.

A climate of hate

Across Europe, newspapers did their best to whip people up into a patriotic fury. Sadly, it worked:

Britain
- The label 'Made in Germany' was introduced in 1887, to encourage people to buy British. In the long run, German manufacturers found it helped sales!

- Children were taught hateful poems such as:

  'Little girls and little boys
  Never suck German toys
  German soldiers licked will make
  Darling Baby's tummy ache.'

- In London's East End, German shops were looted and even German pianos thrown into the road.

- German Shepherd dogs were renamed Alsatians. Later, during the war, Dachshunds were attacked in the streets (for having a German name) or put to sleep by their patriotic owners.

- William Le Queux's novel, *The Invasion of 1910*, which sold over a million copies, created an atmosphere of paranoia and stoked anti-German feelings. It featured Germany, France and Russia joining together to crush

Britain. The idea for the book is said to have come from Field Marshal Earl Roberts, who regularly lectured English schoolboys on the need to prepare for war.

Germany
- All bars, shops and hotels with English or French names were renamed.

- German soldiers chanted the slogan: 'Gott strafe England' (God punish England), a charming catchphrase made up by the poet Ernst Lissauer.

France
- The French tried to rename the perfume eau de Cologne (named after a German town), eau de Provence (after a French region).

Australia
- After the war broke out, 69 Australian towns with German names were renamed. So in 1917, Petersburg (named after German settler Peter Doecke) became Peterborough.

The United States
- Dachshunds were renamed 'liberty dogs', while German measles became 'liberty measles'.

- Libraries across the country destroyed German-language books in public burnings.

- In Illinois, an angry mob lynched Robert Prager, a German coal miner, for hoarding explosives (which were never found).

Trouble had been brewing for many years. Between 1890 and 1914, the great powers had slowly split into two rival gangs. On one side of the European playground were the Central Powers, led by Germany, Austria-Hungary and Turkey. On the other side were France, Russia and Britain.

It all started back in the 1860s, when Germany was made up of 39 small states. The most powerful among them, Prussia, smashed its opponents Austria-Hungary and France, establishing a long-standing gripe in France over the loss of Alsace and Lorraine (a fairly sizeable chunk of territory). By 1871, the Prussian Chancellor Otto von Bismarck convinced other states such as Saxony and Bavaria to join Prussia in forming a single nation, Germany. Together they created a strong, industrial country with a top-notch railway system and a huge, modern army.

Germany was the nervous new kid on the block, looking to make friends and be accepted by the big boys: Britain, France and Russia. Despite their powerful army, the Germans were worried that the French were looking for revenge, so they hooked up with the Austro-Hungarian empire. The two countries also promised to gang up if Russia attacked either of them. In 1882, Italy cosied up to them, forming an alliance known as the Central Powers.[2]

Germany also wanted an empire and a world-class navy to boot, so that nobody would ever dare attack them again. In 1901, the German emperor, Kaiser Wilhelm II, boasted of Germany's colonies, her 'place in the sun', and by 1913 his country had overtaken Britain as Europe's leading industrial power. Britain wasn't particularly bothered about a few Pacific islands and the odd port in China, but they still believed in the words of the old song:

'Rule, Britannia!
Britannia, rule the waves.
Britons never, never, never shall be slaves.'[3]

2. The sly Italians also made a secret pact with the French to stay neutral if Germany invaded France. They waited until May 1915 before coming in on the Allied side.
3. This patriotic British song was actually written by a Scottish poet, James Thomson, in 1740.

Spy mania

Long before the war started, the British were paranoid that German spies lurked in their midst, thanks to scaremongering novels such as *The Battle of Dorking* (1871) by George Tomkyns Chesney, and *The Riddle of the Sands* (1903) by Erskine Childers (who later smuggled German rifles into Ireland to help Irish rebels against England).

- When war broke out, rumours spread of sentries being assaulted, hit-and-run attacks on trains, and secret gun emplacements disguised as tennis courts. A few tennis courts and gardens in London were even dug up and inspected.

- Spy hunting became a national sport. At one stage, 400 people a day were being reported as spies, such as the Swiss waiter accused of sketching military defences. He had simply drawn a seating plan for his restaurant.

- No-one was above suspicion. Lord Haldane, the Secretary of State for War, received sackfuls of hate mail and was jeered in the street after being accused of having a German chauffeur and a dog named Kaiser.

- After a night of drinking aboard HMS *Iron Duke*, Winston Churchill, First Lord of the Admiralty, became convinced that his neighbour, retired MP Arthur Bignold, was signalling to the Germans using a searchlight on the roof of his mansion. He organised a raiding party; Churchill held Bignold and his butler at gunpoint while the house was searched. You guessed it – nothing was found!

- At Maldon in Essex a mob gathered outside a house where a pigeon had landed on the roof, thought to be carrying a secret message. It was simply lost!

- Other rumours told of German planes dropping poisoned sweets, German grocers in England poisoning food, German barbers cutting the throats of their customers, and secret Zeppelin bases in Cumberland. One village in Gloucestershire believed the local blackberry bushes had been poisoned by villainous German saboteurs.

- When he moved to Cornwall, writer D. H. Lawrence was accused of spying for the Germans, purely because his wife was German. The local police even tailed him on country walks and eventually he was banned from Cornwall in 1917 (and from leaving the country).

- Spy mania led to a flood of new plays and novels. Even Sherlock Holmes was brought out of retirement by author Conan Doyle to lock horns with German spymaster Von Bork.

When the German Naval Law of 1898 added another 16 ships to the German fleet, it was a warning shot across the bows of the British Navy.[4] Back on dry land, Germany's growing strength and her Central Powers pals gave France and Russia the collywobbles.[5] To settle their nerves, they joined forces in 1892, leading to the 'Triple Entente' of France, Russia and Britain in 1907. Though this wasn't a strict alliance, it was enough to bring the three together as the Allied Powers in the coming war.

All these nations strengthened their armies and brushed up their war plans. Yet despite the growing tensions, most governments were confident that the sheer size and strength of the two power blocs would prevent war from breaking out. Other countries tagged along – Serbia was linked by treaty to Russia and Bulgaria sided with the Central Powers in 1915.

4. The arms race between Britain and Germany intensified after the launch of HMS Dreadnought in 1906, which was bigger, faster and better armed than any battleship before.
5. It didn't help that the German government was packed with generals.

Most of these agreements weren't meant to last more than a few years, but a series of small bust-ups between 1898 and 1912 drove the partners together. Austria-Hungary, Serbia and the Ottoman Empire squabbled over the Balkans, while the Germans supported the Dutch Boers in South Africa against Britain in 1899–1902. Yet there had been crises before. What was so different?

All over Europe, people eyed each other suspiciously. The British were terrified of a German invasion and saw spies and traitors everywhere. What if the German fleet was waiting to pounce? In France, the generals did the maths – 60 million Germans compared to 40 million Frenchmen – and knew that delaying the war would only benefit Germany, which had a faster-growing population.

The Germans had their own worries. Russia finally updated its army after a humiliating and unexpected defeat by Japan in 1905. The 'sleeping bear' was waking up in other ways. Thanks to enormous French loans, Russia's industrial output was expected to be triple Germany's by 1917. By the winter of 1912,

German army chief Helmuth von Moltke was already restless: 'I think the war is unavoidable – and the sooner the better.'[6] Generals everywhere fretted at the thought of the other side mobilising first, their railway networks whizzing troops to the front.

The clouds of war had begun to gather. It wasn't just professional soldiers who were warming to the idea of a 'short and glorious' war. When it started, this was possibly the most popular war in history.[7] On the continent, millions of young men had already spent time in the army, where they were taught to put king and country first. In Britain, 2.5 million men joined up of their own free will. Many enlisted straight away, no question about it. Huge crowds cheered them on their way as they sped to the front lines. No-one realised just how horrific the war was going to be.[8]

6. *Moltke wasn't the one stirring things up. In the summer of 1914, the Kaiser remarked that 'The whole of Germany is charged with electricity. It only needs a spark to set the whole thing off.'*
7. *Not everyone was thrilled. On 2 August 1914, two days before war was declared, there were scuffles on the streets of London as peace marchers clashed with those who wanted war.*
8. *That said, in 1917 the Americans knew all about the horrors and yet still joined the US Army in their millions.*

The spark

In mid-1914, it took just one little spark to set Europe ablaze. On 26 June, 19-year-old Gavrilo Princip assassinated archduke Franz Ferdinand, the future emperor of Austria-Hungary. The archduke and his wife Sophie were in Sarajevo on an official tour of Bosnia (as well as celebrating their wedding anniversary). At the time, though Bosnia was part of the Austro-Hungarian empire, most Serbs thought it should belong to Serbia. The Black Hand, a Serbian secret society,[9] came up with a clever wheeze: let's kill the archduke, and if we recruit a few eager students to do our dirty work, no-one can pin it on us.

The first attempt was made by Nedeljko Čabrinović, who threw a grenade at the archduke's car. It simply rolled off the back and wounded several unlucky bystanders. A furious Franz Ferdinand cancelled that afternoon's army inspection. But no-one told his driver. Taking a wrong turn after lunch,

9. Many of its members were serving military officers – even the Serbian Crown Prince Alexander was a supporter. The plan was put together by Colonel Dragutin Dimitrijević, nicknamed 'the Bee', who was head of spying in the Serb army.

Georgie, Nicky and Willy

King George V of England, Tsar Nicholas II of Russia and Kaiser Wilhelm II were all grandsons of British Queen Victoria, the 'grandmama' of Europe. Surely they could halt the madness? During July and early August 1914 a flurry of telegrams passed between the cousins, but they could do little to stop the move to war as alliances clicked into place and hearts swelled with national pride.

the driver pulled into a narrow street, where Princip just happened to be waiting. He shot from point-blank range. Both the duke and his wife were dead within minutes. To escape capture, Princip tried to kill himself by swallowing cyanide, while one of the other assassins tried to jump in the river.[10] Both were grabbed by an angry mob and handed to the police. But the damage had been done.[11]

10. Gavrilo Princip was too young to be executed. He was put in prison, and died from lung disease just before the end of the war.
11. The archduke's blood-splattered coat can still be seen in the Military History Museum in Vienna.

The assassination of Franz Ferdinand

The Austrians blamed Serbia for the killing, and told Serbia to root out the Black Hand – or face invasion. Presented with this stark ultimatum, the Serbians grovelled but refused to follow every last demand, backed by the their fellow Slavs, the Russians.[12] Due to the complex web of European alliances, within just six weeks this local crisis had spiralled into a European war.

Let's take it step by step:

1. **The Austrians were spooked by the Russian support of Serbia, and turned to their big brother Germany for help. The Germans, happy to risk a large-scale war with Russia, issued the so-called 'blank cheque' on 5–6 July, offering to support Austria-Hungary to the hilt.**

12. *Not everyone felt sorry for the Serbs. The British government thought they were a dangerous bunch, and Prime Minister Herbert Asquith even said privately that they 'deserved a good thrashing'.*

2. The Austrians declared war on the Serbs on 28 July, even though their chief-of-staff Count Franz Conrad von Hötzendorf privately admitted 'It will be a hopeless fight,' as his army was in such poor shape and so many soldiers were on leave to help bring in the harvest.

3. On 31 July, the Russian army moved into position, ready to help the Serbs. The next day, 1 August, the Germans declared war on Russia. When the French mobilised their troops in support of the Russians, the Germans declared war on them too.

4. The Germans hoped to knock out France before Russia had a chance to fully mobilise its army, banking on the fact that it had a poor railway network. But this cunning plan had a fatal flaw – German troops would have to march through neutral Belgium. The Germans gambled that Britain would ignore the mere 'scrap of paper' that made them allies with Belgium. They were wrong. On 4 August 1914, Britain entered a full-scale war for the first time since the Crimean War, some sixty years earlier.

The war was truly off and running, and for the first few months, it certainly felt like a race as the big powers rushed to get their troops into battle.

10 smaller nations that joined the war (—)

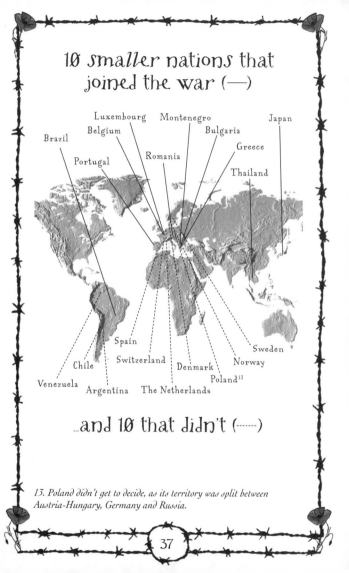

Luxembourg   Montenegro   Japan

Belgium   Bulgaria

Brazil   Greece

Portugal   Romania   Thailand

Spain   Sweden

Chile   Switzerland   Norway

Venezuela   Denmark

Argentina   The Netherlands   Poland[13]

...and 10 that didn't (-----)

13. Poland didn't get to decide, as its territory was split between Austria-Hungary, Germany and Russia.

The Sopwith Camel could achieve a top speed of 113 mph (182 km/h).

Tally-ho!

The 1917 Sopwith Camel gained **more** combat victories (1,294) than any other type of fighter plane.

CHAPTER TWO

INTO BATTLE (1914)

The first shots of the war were fired by Austria-Hungary on 28 July 1914, when their gunboats began lobbing shells at the Serb capital of Belgrade. At this point, the Austrians thought they were heading into another Balkan war that would be done and dusted once they swatted away the Serb army. They didn't feel so big or clever two days later, when the Russian army carried through its threat to go to war. The Balkan war was now a European one.

Like it or not, many of the young men of Europe had already served in their country's armed forces for a few years. Known as conscription, or 'the draft', this system meant that as soon as war was declared, huge reserves of trained soldiers could be called up by France, Germany, Austria and Russia. The odd man out was Britain, which unlike the other European powers did not have a large standing army – its real strength was its world-beating navy.

At the start of the war, speed was everything: every nation raced to get their troops equipped and delivered to the front lines in the quickest possible time (known as 'mobilising'). For the next four years, Europe rang with the sound of clattering trains as soldiers were shuttled to and fro. In France, people joked that the men were eaten by the Gare de l'Est (East Station), as so many of the soldiers who kipped on its platforms before heading off to the trenches never returned.

For the Germans, this was going to be a war fought by timetable. Army chief Helmuth von Moltke gave himself just 40 days to conquer France. Following the Schlieffen plan, his forces were expected to waltz through Belgium, then 'take a stroll to Paris'.

Huns, hairy beasts and Tommies

- To Germans, a front-line foot soldier was a *Frontschwein*, or 'front pig'. To the French, he was a *poilu*, or 'hairy beast'. To almost everyone, a British soldier was a 'Tommy'. This was short for Tommy Atkins, a name first used by the War Office to describe a typical soldier in a booklet published in 1815.

- Meanwhile the Germans called their French counterparts *Franzmann* and names based on French phrases such as *Olala* and *Palewuhs* (parlez-vous). In return, the French called Germans *Boche* or *Fritz*.

- At the start of the war, the British used 'Fritz' to describe the Germans, with 'Jerry' used later on. The word 'Hun', made up by the papers, was used mostly by British officers.

- Australians called themselves 'Diggers', an old nickname revived after the ANZACs (Australian and New Zealand Army Corps) had to dig themselves into the cliffs at Gallipoli, Turkey (see page 85).

- On 24 May 1915, a short truce was declared at Gallipoli to bury the dead. Australian and Turkish troops got to know each other. From then on, the ANZACs considered the Turks more like sporting rivals than enemies, calling them 'Jacko', 'Abdul' or 'Johnnie Turk'.

The Belgian army had other ideas, putting up a stiff fight in the forts around Liège that slowed the Germans down. So did a few 'free shooters', Belgian civilians who couldn't resist taking pot shots at the invaders.

The Germans took harsh measures to stamp out any opposition, rounding up hostages and shooting them, or carrying out random acts of violence to terrify people into submission. One of the worst massacres happened in the town of Dinant on 23 August 1914.

Shock tactics

In the first weeks of the war, a million Belgians crossed the border to neutral Holland. Realising that a border patrol would tie up valuable troops needed on the front line, in spring 1915 the Germans built a 3-metre-high electric fence between occupied Belgium and the Netherlands. The 2,000-volt wire ran almost 200 km through villages, orchards, meadows, and even across the width of the River Meuse. Yet the refugees kept on coming, and some 3,000 people are thought to have been killed attempting to cross the border.

German troops were hit by a few stray shots fired by French troops on the other side of the River Meuse. Blaming the locals, they rounded up 674 people and executed them. This played into the hands of the Allied propaganda machine, which leapt on any story that made the 'Huns' look barbaric.

Meanwhile, on 7 August, the four divisions (about 100,000 men) of the British Expeditionary Force (BEF) had crossed to France to halt the German advance. Further south, the French launched Plan 17, hoping to win back Alsace-Lorraine in a lightning attack. It seemed just like the good old days, with armies moving rapidly across large battlefields. Many still had cavalry units dressed in colourful outfits from the previous century. But while the uniforms and equipment of the average foot soldier had changed little in 30 years, few generals had cottoned on to the fact that modern weapons were incredibly efficient at killing people:

- **Rifles now had a range of a mile (1.6 km) or more and fired 10 rounds a minute, while many machine guns could fire 400–600.**

- In 1897, the French came up with the first quick-firing big artillery, which could fire over 20 rounds (shells) in a minute.

- The invention of smokeless powder in the 1880s meant that the firer could remain hidden.

All of this meant that the odds were heavily stacked in favour of the defender. It was soon clear that the rules of warfare had changed forever. For all their gallantry, attackers were cut down in swathes by a hail of machine-gun bullets and thudding shells. The French troops suffered worse than most, their blue jackets and red trousers making them easy targets.[1] In just the first month of the war, France lost over 200,000 men, including 40 per cent of their officers. Soon they were forced to retreat while Paris, their capital, was in serious danger.

By 23 August 1914, the BEF were grouped around the Belgian town of Mons. Though outnumbered three to one, they held off the advancing German troops for 48 hours.

1. To make matters worse, they were bogged down by heavy kit, including a large and rather cumbersome rifle, the 8 mm Lebel.

The Russians are coming

The outbreak of war led to all sorts of wild stories. One told how Russian regiments were passing through Britain on their way to fight in France. Reports poured in of landings in Scotland, troops in railway stations stamping Siberian snow off their boots, and rough fellows with beards, cigars and fur hats calling rudely for vodka or jamming slot machines with Russian coins.

By September 1914, the rumours were being published as fact by US newspapers, who told of hundreds of thousands of Russian troops in Britain. The British government kept schtum, hoping to fool German commanders into believing there might be an attack any day on the Belgian coast. The story may even have helped the Allies during the defence of Paris, as German troops were sent north to defend the coast.

Cossack in the Russian cavalry

Tall tales

During the Great War, governments would say anything to make their enemies out to be monsters, and newspapers, always happy to print a shocking headline, were expected to publish what the government wanted. Big whoppers printed by British newspapers included:

OUTRAGE: BELGIAN CHILD'S HANDS CUT OFF BY GERMANS.

HORROR: GERMANS CRUCIFY CANADIAN OFFICER.

ATROCITY: GERMAN SOLDIERS PARADE ROUND BELGIAN TOWNS WITH BABIES ON THEIR BAYONETS.

ANGER: BELGIAN MONKS KILLED AFTER REFUSING TO RING THE CHURCH BELLS OF ANTWERP TO CELEBRATE THE GERMAN OCCUPATION OF THE CITY. THE GERMANS STRAP THEM TO THE HAMMERS THEN RING THE BELLS, CRUSHING THE POOR MONKS.

Similarly, German headlines read:

SCANDAL: FRENCH DOCTORS INFECT GERMAN WELLS WITH PLAGUE GERMS

SHOCK: GERMAN PRISONERS
BLINDED BY ALLIED CAPTORS

It was all nonsense, of course, but sadly, the bigger the lie, the more people were willing to believe it:

- The British government spread a story in 1917 that the Germans had built a factory near Coblenz that boiled down the fat from dead soldiers and used it to make soap, pig food and explosives. Though a complete and utter porkie pie (lie), it helped to persuade China to join the war on the side of the Allies, and also gave a huge boost to the number of soldiers who joined the US army.

- In 1914, British Army HQ concocted an order, supposedly from the Kaiser himself, which read:

My soldiers to exterminate first the treacherous English; walk over Field Marshal French's contemptible little Army.

It angered the BEF troops so much that they renamed themselves the 'Old Contemptibles'.

The British defence of Mons was helped by rifle fire so rapid that the Germans thought they were facing batteries of machine guns.[2] But when the French were forced to retreat, the BEF had no choice but to fall back too. So began the epic retreat from Mons.[3] For 12 days, the BEF fought off the pursuing Germans, with little food or rest until they finally dug in east of Paris on 6 September.

The grim reality of modern war must have come as a great shock to troops on both sides. This was war like never before. Whole regiments took to their heels[4] and the roads of northern France were clogged with fleeing soldiers and refugees pushing carts of prized possessions. In the east, the Russians got themselves sorted far quicker than the Germans expected, and by 4 August they were marching into East Prussia where there was only a small German army. A startled

2. The Germans also made the mistake of advancing at first in close 'parade ground' formations, providing easy targets for the well-trained British riflemen.
3. The British revel in glorious failures: think of the Charge of the Light Brigade during the Crimean war, the evacuation from Gallipoli (see page 85), or the evacuation from Dunkirk in World War II.
4. Fleeing troops were severely punished by the French; 600 soldiers were shot for desertion, many of them in 1914.

Moltke gave the order to switch 100,000 troops from the Western Front, just as the Germans reached the outskirts of Paris. The French government fled, along with a million Parisians. Despite the danger, the French and British commanders squabbled – British commander Sir John French blamed his heavy losses on the sudden French retreat and threatened to withdraw the BEF from the battlefield.

Wisely, the French Commander-in-Chief Joseph Joffre stepped in to patch things up and the Allied troops dug in along the River Marne. When the Germans tried to outflank the French, Joffre seized his opportunity and counter-attacked, helped by thousands of troops who had hitched a ride to the front line in 600 Parisian taxi cabs. Fresh from the training ground and with full bellies,[5] they faced hungry German troops worn out after marching over 240 km in a few weeks.

Within a week, the Allies had won the Battle of the Marne and over four days the Germans were forced to retreat almost 65 kilometres.

5. *Never underestimate the importance of a full belly in war. As Napoleon himself once declared: 'An army marches on its stomach.'*

Poor General von Moltke suffered a nervous breakdown, and is said to have told the Kaiser: 'Your Majesty, we have lost the war.' As it turned out, he wasn't far wrong.

Home for Christmas?

Each side tried in vain to outflank the other, creating a 'race to the sea' as troops were hurriedly ferried north by railway. Each and every move led to another small battle and extended the battlefront along a wider and wider line. When the dust settled, it was clear that no-one was going anywhere.

With the Schlieffen Plan a dead duck, the Germans dug in. By early 1915, a continuous line of trenches snaked over 765 kilometres from northern France down to the Swiss border, guarded by millions of soldiers. The Germans held the best positions on high ground,[6] while the Allies were forced to dig in opposite. The earth was often rock-hard, resulting in shallower trenches.

6. The German attack on France had also captured nearly 75 per cent of all French coal and 80 per cent of their pig iron, along with the ports of Belgium, which were ideal as bases for the German submarine fleet.

The German Kaiser told his troops as they left for the front in August 1914: 'You will be home before the leaves have fallen from the trees.' Millions of schoolteachers, postmen and factory workers all over Europe had joined up expecting to be back at work by Christmas. But the quick knockout turned into a long, bloody slugging match. In 1815, Waterloo was fought and won in a day, but in 1914–18 each battle lasted for months (there was no break for winter) and the casualties kept on piling up. The Germans hoped to grind the Allies down, while the Allies hoped for a mighty breakthrough that would take them all the way to Berlin.

For most of the next four years, the battlefields of Belgium and France (known as the Western Front) were clearly marked by rows of trenches and barbed wire. In fact, both sides dug a bewildering maze of ditches, tunnels and dugouts. They didn't run in a straight line, but were built in short zig-zagging sections that protected soldiers from a direct hit further along the line.[7]

7. Including all the zigs and zags and reserve trenches on both sides, the trench systems along the Western Front were about 32,000 km long in total.

Seven steps to slaughter

During the winter and spring of 1914–15 the French made the first attempt to break the stalemate on the Western Front, in a mass attack that aimed to smash through the German lines. Despite the ferocious slaughter, this tactic was used repeatedly over the next three years. Here's how it worked from the viewpoint of a general:

1. The night before, mass your troops in their thousands along the front line.

2. For hours (or days) before, pound the enemy lines with shells. In theory this should kill plenty of the enemy and clear the barbed wire (though as you are about to find out, it doesn't do either).

3. Attack! First your troops have to climb out of trenches, known as going 'over the top'. (Ladders are usually required.)

4. Then order them to walk calmly across no man's land in long lines as the bullets whizz about their ears. Officers should lead from the front. No running or clever zigzags allowed as this will only cause confusion (or so you think).

5. Due to the smoke and exploding shells, by now you have probably lost sight of your men. Your only hope of passing on fresh

orders is by sending a runner. This takes time – and more often than not the unlucky so-and-so gets shot before the message is delivered (not that you find out until it's too late).

6. Don't be surprised if enemy shells or machine-gun fire make mincemeat of your men. If by some miracle they make it across no man's land and capture the enemy trench, don't panic. Chances are you won't have to think about what to do next as the enemy will counter-attack quickly enough and retake the trench.

7. If anyone questions your tactics, politely explain that you never expected the attack to actually break through. After all, this is a war of attrition and in the long run the enemy should run out of troops (who are still standing) before you do.

Trench hospitals were set up on the battlefield to give immediate treatment, although it was sometimes impossible to provide anything more than first aid.

Trench talk

The trench at the front was known as the 'fire trench'. Behind this there were usually two or more lines of 'support' or 'reserve' trenches, somewhere to fall back to in case of attack. These were linked by 'communication' trenches that allowed supplies and fresh troops to be brought to the fire trench. At night, sentries kept watch in trenches called 'saps', dead-ends that led out into no man's land, the gap between the opposing sides.

The German trenches were the best: deep and lined with concrete. They were also built close to railway lines so they were easy to supply. By comparison, many of the first Allied trenches were little more than pits joined together. Even by the summer of 1915, when it was clear they weren't going anywhere fast, the British and French trenches were so shallow that their troops had to keep their heads down as they walked along. It seems crazy, but British troops were only given steel helmets in 1916 (which – surprise, surprise – reduced head wounds by 75 per cent).

Daily routine in the trenches

The day began with a 'Stand-to (Arms)' at dawn. Each man would be expected to stand on the trench fire step, rifle loaded, bayonet fixed. Tommies called this the 'morning hate' as both sides often relieved the tension by blasting machine gun and rifle fire into the mist (just to be on the safe side). An hour or so later, during the 'breakfast truce', one man was left on guard duty while his section had breakfast and a tot of rum. Then it was time to catch forty winks, if you weren't disturbed by an inspection. At dusk, there was another 'Stand-to' before the night duties began.

Many soldiers died as they struggled to get over or through a relatively new invention: barbed wire.

Life in the trenches

At any time, only part of the army was on the front line, and the usual period of duty was just four to six days. But even in the reserve trenches the battles against hunger, the weather and the lack of sleep continued.[8]

- **Wastage.** Don't blame the trenches – the real danger came when troops stepped out of them to go on the attack (or had to run away). Even so, enemy snipers picked off dozens of men each day, which the army politely referred to as 'natural wastage'.

- **Rain.** The low-lying fields of Belgium and Northern France meant that trenches soon filled with water, becoming stinking seas of mud mixed with human waste (for toilets most soldiers used buckets or the nearest shell-hole).

- **Food.** A big moan among soldiers on both sides. British troops hated the tins of bully beef (canned corned beef), but enjoyed maconochie (a stew of meat, sliced turnips and carrots). Other rations included hard biscuits and jam (which for some reason was always plum and apple). The French soldiers were given hard mint sweets.

8. Though many senior officers did die on the front lines, they certainly enjoyed a more luxurious lifestyle – some lived in country houses far behind the lines where they enjoyed shooting parties, horse riding and fine dining. French Commander-In-Chief at the beginning of the war, General Joseph Joffre, expected a two-hour lunch every day.

- **Cold.** Most dugouts had a brazier where coal could be lit to warm hands or food. But in winter, frostbite was a real hazard. To keep warm, soldiers were given tins of anti-frostbite grease. They were expected to strip off their clothes and smear their bodies in the fat. Not surprisingly, many refused.

- **Disease** (see page 130). In almost all previous wars, more soldiers died from disease than from wounds, and disease remained a huge problem in the trenches. The heavily manured soil of northern France often led to the spread of gangrene, meaning that even minor leg wounds could kill.

- **Sores and blisters.** To prevent blisters, soldiers urinated in their boots to soften them up. As urine is a good antiseptic, it also prevented trench foot (see page 130).

- **Sheer boredom.** Most of the year was spent preparing for attack, taking turns at sentry duty and digging. The men filled idle moments with jokes, singing and games of cards (though gambling was officially banned).

- **Getting along.** Inevitably soldiers got on each other's nerves. But everyone was expected to 'muck in', which meant looking out for others. Even so, some regiments were unpopular. The British Royal Army Medical Corps (RAMC), were nicknamed 'Rob All My Comrades' as soldiers suspected they emptied the pockets of dead men.

In the dead of night

Bizarrely, soldiers in the trenches were often busiest at night, hidden by the dark from the prying eyes of pilots and balloon observers spotting above. Many dozed during the day instead.

- At night, the battlefield was pitch-black, and silent except for the croaking of frogs, the occasional hoot of an owl and the distant boom of the big guns.

- It was a good time to repair trenches and holes in the barbed wire, and to bring stores such as sandbags up to the fire trench.

- Total silence was a must. Tools were muffled with cloths and soldiers communicated with hand signals. Everyone had to dive for cover if no man's land was lit up by flares (whoever set them off).

- Some teams were sent out to collect the dead and wounded. Other squads tried to capture prisoners or 'booty' – letters and other documents – to learn the enemy's battle plans.

- Night attacks were carried out by troops armed with a positively medieval selection of knives, clubs, knuckle-dusters and hatchets as well as rifles and bayonets. Wearing woollen caps and with faces darkened with burnt cork, the raiders looked like pirates.

Extra cover was provided by sandbags at the front of the trench, the 'parapet', and also at the back, to protect from shells exploding behind. Periscopes were often used to watch the enemy without the risk of getting shot by a sniper.

The trenches were also protected by a sea of razor-sharp barbed wire. On the German side these were up to 90 metres wide, and a heavy bombardment simply turned the wire into a jumbled mess rather than cutting through it. Even at the best of times, it was very hard to cut by hand (some rifles were fitted with wirecutters at the end of the barrel). During an attack, soldiers often got entangled in the wire, making them easy targets for enemy fire.

No wonder it was almost impossible for foot soldiers to cross no man's land without being cut to ribbons. As a result, by the end of 1917 the trenches on the Western Front were pretty much back to where they had been three years before. Had your fill of trenches? Then let's get back to the action.

In October 1914, General Erich von Falkenhayn, the new German commander, made a valiant attempt to break the stalemate by attacking the British at Ypres. This time it was the brave German attackers who were cut down as they charged across the open fields. Within a month, the First Battle of Ypres ground to a halt as heavy rains turned the battlefield into a mudbath and supplies of ammunition ran low.

You may have heard a far-fetched story that groups of soldiers from both sides met in no man's land and celebrated Christmas together. Amazingly, it's true. Often these truces started with a plea to bury dead comrades lying between the trenches; one German historian claims it began after German soldiers lobbed chocolate cake at British troops instead of hand grenades. Not only English and German but French, Belgian, Austrian and Russian soldiers took part. Soldiers swapped gifts and addresses, drank together, and even played kickabout games of football. This was frowned on by the generals, and the troops were told they'd be shot if this sort of thing happened again.

Creature discomforts

In the trenches you were never alone:

- **Rats.** There were rats (and frogs) everywhere. They ate soldiers' rations and spread disease, and some grew large feasting on unburied corpses. They soon got used to having people around, and scrambled over men as they snoozed in the trenches. The troops fought back with guns and clubs. It was a never-ending battle, but at least it relieved the boredom.

- **Lice.** Over 95 per cent of all soldiers in the trenches were affected by tiny critters called lice, which left red blotches on the victim's body. Worse, they spread nasty diseases like trench fever and typhus. Clean water was in short supply, so comrades gathered in groups to pick off the lice, known as 'chatting'. German soldiers used to drop lice onto a heated tin lid so they could listen to them sizzling as they burned.

- **Flies.** They were attracted to the dead bodies in giant swarms. According to one German officer, they were so thick on the ground they looked like a cushion of velvet. In Gallipoli an Australian soldier wrote:
'Some of them must have tin openers for feet, they bite so hard.'

While we're on the subject, this wasn't the first time this sort of chumminess broke out. During lulls in fighting during the Crimean War (1854–1856) British and French soldiers gathered around the same fire, smoking and drinking (and Cossack dancing?) with their Russian enemies. In the American Civil War (1861–1865), Union and Confederate soldiers traded tobacco, coffee and newspapers, fished peacefully along the same stream and even collected blackberries together.

There's more! On at least one occasion, First World War defenders suddenly stopped shooting and told the enemy to head back to the safety of their own lines. Apparently a battery of Austrian machine gunners had shot so many Italians that the next wave of attackers could hardly climb over the mountain of dead comrades. It's said that the Austrians stopped firing and shouted out: 'Stop, go back! We won't shoot any more. Do you all want to die?'

Not all the Austrians were quite so gallant, it has to be said. The Austro-Hungarian forces that waded into Serbia at the beginning of the

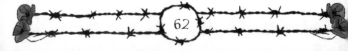

war showed no mercy, massacring some 4,000 civilians during the opening invasion and looting everything in sight after their supplies ran out.

Though the Austrians captured the Serbian capital, Belgrade, the Serbs fought back bravely, even though there weren't enough rifles to go around and only a third of their troops could be moved by train; the rest had to walk all the way on foot. By December 1914, the Austrians had been driven out of Serbia. To the northeast, in Galicia (a region now split between Poland and Ukraine), the Russian forces pushed the Austrians back so fast they were forced to abandon 1,000 steam locomotives and 15,000 wagons. By the spring of 1915, 120,000 Austrian troops besieged at Przemyśl had surrendered. In less than a year, Austria had already lost 957,000 men. For what? Stalemate on two fronts. No wonder a German general bitterly complained his country was 'shackled to a corpse'.

That said, the Austrians had done a good job of sucking in the Russian forces. The Germans' counter-attack in East Prussia

caught the Russians on the hop, helped by poor Russian radio equipment. In fact, it was so shockingly bad, the Russians resorted to openly broadcasting their battle plans in Morse Code (which everybody knew). The astonished Germans who listened in to these messages drew the Russians into a huge trap near the town of Tannenberg, resulting in a crushing victory.[9] A second hammer blow a few days later at the First Battle of the Masurian Lakes stopped the Russian advance in its tracks.

If all this seems a lot more dramatic than the drudgery of the trenches in the west, it's worth noting that the Eastern Front, which stretched from the Baltic to the Black Sea, was twice as long as the Western Front. As a result, there was a lot more wriggle room for even the biggest armies.

9. The Okhrana, the Russian secret service, shifted the blame for the defeat onto the Minister for War. Apparently he had given away the plans in a letter to a friend in Austria. The Okhrana argued that the phrase 'long walks are out of the question' (due to the bad weather) was a coded message!

War on the seven seas

While on land everyone was getting terribly bogged down, at sea the British and German fleets played a nervous game of cat-and-mouse, though it's hard to say who was the cat and who was the mouse. On the one hand, the British fleet was still by far the largest in the world. On the other, the German fleet had newer battleships and more submarines, or 'U-boats' (short for *Unterseeboot*) as the Germans called them.

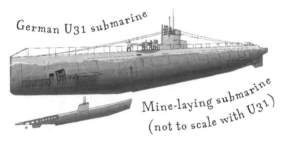

German U31 submarine

Mine-laying submarine (not to scale with U31)

'Vessels of every kind...have been sent ruthlessly to the bottom without warning or thought of help.'

President Woodrow Wilson describes the German U-boat campaign.

During the first year of the war, there was no titanic battle between the fleets. But the British did begin to close off the North Sea. This tactic, known as a blockade, prevented German shipping from reaching the rest of the world. As you will see, it became more and more important the longer the war dragged on.

The only downside of the blockade was that it left the English east coast open to attack by German warships. On 16 December 1914, The First High Seas Scouting Group (forget woggles and scarves, this was a group of

Grandad's army

The trenches were filled with the elderly as well as the young: Lieutenant Henry Webber died at the Battle of the Somme in July 1916, aged 67. (He had three sons serving, all of whom outranked him.) Chief Gunner Israel Harding, another winner of the Victoria Cross, had his left leg broken when his ship was blown up during the Gallipoli campaign. He was 84 years old and had fought in the Crimean War in 1853–1856!

fast, powerful battleships) bombarded coastal towns such as Scarborough, Hartlepool and Whitby. After an outcry in the press, the Royal Navy finally managed to catch up with the raiding party a month later in the North Sea. One German battleship was sunk and another was badly damaged in the skirmish, putting a stop to further raids.

In the days before radar, it wasn't that easy to track down an enemy fleet. But throughout the war, the British had an ace up their sleeve – a copy of the Germany Navy's codebook. A special unit under spymaster William 'Blinker' Hall, known as Room 40, listened in to German chatter as they reported where they were, and what they were up to.

A global war

While the big guns were churning up the battlefields of Europe, the clash of empires meant that by the end of 1914 the fighting had spread to the Far East, South Atlantic, Africa, Central Asia and Middle East.

Boy soldiers

Most armies in the Great War used child soldiers. When the war started, the enthusiasm to join up meant that young boys (and even girls) queued up alongside their elder brothers. These teenagers were sent to the front lines in Belgium, France, Russia and Turkey, where they fought alongside older soldiers – and died with them.

- The story goes that underage teenagers wishing to enlist used to write the number '18' on a piece of paper which they then placed inside their shoe. This meant that if a recruiting officer asked them if they were 'over 18', they could answer 'yes' in all honesty!

- Many recruiting officers were happy to turn a blind eye and the British army refused to ask recruits to show their birth certificate. However, eventually the army did allow parents to bring underage soldiers back home.

- John Condon from Waterford, Ireland, was said to have been just 12 years old when he joined the Royal Irish Regiment. He died on 24 May 1915, during a German gas attack near Ypres. Private James Bartaby joined up aged 13 years and 10 months. He was wounded and got sent home in October 1915.

- Teenager Jack Cornwell won a Victoria Cross, Britain's highest military honour, during the Battle of Jutland in June 1916. After his ship HMS *Chester* was hit by German shells, he stayed at his post even though the rest of his gun crew were dead and he'd been badly wounded. He died aged just 16 years and 4 months, before his mother could make it to the hospital to hold her boy for one last time. Though the English newspapers made a big splash out of heroic sacrifice, his family were soon forgotten (his mother died in poverty in 1919).

- US Senator Mike Mansfield was a boy soldier during the Great War. In 1917, he quit school at 14 and tried to enlist, but was turned down. He got hold of a copy of his birth certificate and changed the date to make himself older. He joined the Navy and crossed the Atlantic seven times before the truth came out and he was sent home.

- After travelling through Russia in 1916–1917, travel writer Stephen Graham (1884–1975) wrote that:

'*There is scarcely a town or school from which boys have not run away to the war.*'

He added:

'*Hundreds of Russian girls have gone off in boy's clothes and tried to pass themselves off as boys and enlist as volunteers.*'

The Ottoman Empire, ruled by the Turks, joined the war in November 1914, after two German victories over the Russians hinted that they were the team to back.[10]

The Turks saw the war as a great opportunity to regain lost territories in the Balkans and North Africa and to conquer new lands. With an army of some 600,000 troops, Turkey represented a serious threat to the British Empire. When the Ottoman Sultan Mehmed V declared a Holy War against the Allies, the British wasted no time in landing a force in Mesopotamia (now Iraq) to protect a major oil pipeline.

Within weeks, the Turks struck back with a surprise attack on the Suez Canal, a vital sea route used to ship supplies and soldiers from India and Australia to Europe. They were supported by the Germans, who hoped to stir up the Muslims and Arabs in revolt against the British and French.[11] But there was no Holy War, and the British defended Suez, inflicting heavy losses on the Turks.

10. The Turks had already signed a treaty with Germany, in August 1914. It was so hush-hush that only five people knew about it in Turkey.
11. Conspirators in the US also supplied arms to revolutionaries in India, but again the hoped-for rebellion against British rule never happened.

In the early months of the war, the Turks also conducted a disastrous campaign against the Russians. Around 30,000 Turkish troops froze to death in blizzards before they even fired a shot. The Turks took their anger out on the Armenians. In the spring of 1915, Turkish troops forced millions of Armenians from their homes. Those who survived the trek across the Sinai desert died in prison camps in Aleppo, Syria. Over a million Armenians were killed in perhaps the first example of modern genocide – another inglorious first for the Great War.

Waves from the European war rippled all over the planet. In China, a joint Japanese and British force captured the German port of Tsingtao. Forced to head out to sea, a fleet led by German Admiral Maximilian Graf von Spee wreaked havoc on British shipping in the Indian and Pacific Oceans, capturing 23 merchant ships. A short while later, on 1 November 1914, von Spee defeated a British fleet off the coast of Chile.

This made a mockery of the Royal Navy's boast that it ruled the waves. Two of Britain's biggest battleships, HMS *Invincible* and HMS

Inflexible, were immediately dispatched to ambush the German fleet off the Falkland Islands. Four of von Spee's cruisers were sunk and the brave admiral was one of 2,200 German sailors who went down with their ships.

There were also early successes for the British in Africa, where a rebellion by the Dutch Boers in support of the Germans was soon put down by forces led by General Jan Smuts. Smuts then took the South African army into the German colony of South West Africa. Though his troops faced land mines and poisoned wells, by May 1915 most of the country was in British hands.

At the same time, a naval war was being fought in German East Africa between Germany and Belgium to control Africa's most strategic waterway, Lake Tanganyika. The British navy sent two small steam-powered gunboats. These were hauled by African porters through jungles and marshes, arriving at the lake in November 1915. A month later, the two gunboats, HMS *Mini* and HMS *Tou Tou*, captured a much larger German gunboat, the *Kingani*, and renamed it HMS *Fifi*![12]

But it wasn't all plain sailing for the Brits. The previous December, 8,000 Indian troops led by British commanders had been ambushed by the Germans. Though both sides were forced to flee by swarms of angry bees, the Germans won the day. They were led by the energetic Colonel Paul Emil von Lettow-Vorbeck, who strengthened his small German force with several thousand tribesmen organised into units known as *ruga-rugas*.

Von Lettow-Vorbeck was a master of hit-and-run attacks, and by the end of the war he is said to have tied up over a million Allied troops. The Africans themselves had little or nothing to gain from the war. Yet so many farmers were forced to act as porters for the colonial armies that the harvest failed, and hundreds of thousands of civilians died in the resulting famine. The European war was now truly a 'world' war, with battles being fought all over the planet.

12. *Inspiring C. S. Forester's classic novel* The African Queen *(1935) and the film of the same name (1951), starring Humphrey Bogart (who won an Oscar) and Katherine Hepburn.*

Animal heroes

- In October 1918, a group of 194 US soldiers were surrounded on all sides by German forces. Their only hope of escape was to send a carrier pigeon with a message tied to its leg. Cher Ami (whose name means 'Dear Friend' in French) flew the 40 kilometres back to the American HQ in just 25 minutes, even though it was shot through the chest by a German bullet. The US troops were rescued and Cher Ami was awarded the Croix de Guerre (with Palm) by the French.

- Marquis, a faithful French messenger dog, collapsed from bullet wounds at the feet of a group of French soldiers after bringing his message across no man's land.

- The most decorated dog of the Great War was the mascot of the US 102nd Infantry, Sergeant Stubby, who took part in 17 battles. He is best known for grabbing a German spy by the seat of his pants after hearing a noise in the dark. When the spy tried to run for it, Stubby tripped him up then hung on until his handler Corporal Robert Conroy arrived on the scene.

The animal army

Animals have been used in battle for almost as long as there have been armies. One story tells how the ancient Persians, knowing how much the Egyptians cared about cats, rounded up as many stray cats as they could then set them loose on the battlefield. The Egyptians couldn't bear the thought of harming the poor moggies, and promptly surrendered. The soldiers of the Great War weren't quite so caring: on the Western Front alone an estimated 250,000 horses died.

These animals suffered just like the troops; blasted by artillery fire, maimed by poison gas, or drowned in the mud.

- **Horses and mules**
  Most armies had cavalry forces at the beginning of the war. Though they had little impact on the Western Front, they had more success in the wide open spaces of the Middle East. But there was no better way of bringing supplies through muddy, difficult terrain than on the backs of horses and mules.[13] Lighter horses were also used for scouting, carrying messages and pulling ambulances, while large Shire horses were teamed together to pull the heavy artillery.[14] Towards the end of the war, thousands of German horses died of starvation due to the lack of fodder.

13. By the end of the war, over a million horses and mules were in service with the British army alone.
14. But as the guns got bigger and bigger, tractors and even locomotives were needed to pull them.

- **Camels**

In 1916, the British created the Imperial Camel Corps (ICC), which fought in the Sinai desert and Palestine campaign. In April 1918, a company of Australian soldiers in the ICC ran out of hand grenades while defending a hill. They resorted to heaving boulders down upon the attacking Turks and eventually fought them off. The hill affectionately became known as the 'Camel's Hump'. The men of the ICC were celebrated in a poem by the Australian writer, Oliver 'Trooper Bluegum' Hogue, who served with the Corps:

> Timothy Hogg was a bold Camelier
> From the land of the setting sun;
> And the girls gave Timmy a rousing cheer
> When he started to mop up the Hun.
>
> He trekked over Egypt and Sinai;
> He led the Jacko's [Turks] a dance,
> And he gleefully cried, as he winked his eye:
> 'I'm lucky I'm not in France.'

- **Elephants**

A few solitary elephants helped with the war effort. One elephant was photographed working for the Germans in occupied France, a gift from a patriotic circus owner. Circus elephants were also used to pull coal carts from railway stations, while another worked in a munitions factory in Sheffield, England.

- **Dogs and cats**
  War dogs had all sorts of uses. Many were
  guard dogs. They also made good messengers,
  as they were smaller and faster than soldiers
  (though female dogs were sometimes used to
  distract enemy hounds). Dogs were used by
  both sides to find wounded soldiers, with a
  first-aid package strapped to their throat,
  while other dogs laid telephone cables across
  the battlefield. The Belgians used big dogs to
  haul batteries of machine guns, as they were
  easier to hide from enemy fire than horses.
  Terriers were used by the British to kill rats
  in the trenches, while the Germans used cats.
  They also provided an early-warning system
  as they became restless if they smelled gas in
  the wind.

- **Pigeons and parrots**
  Over 100,000 carrier pigeons were used in
  the war, and more than nine times out of ten
  they reached their destination with their
  message. Parrots were kept in the Eiffel
  Tower in Paris to warn of approaching
  aircraft. They could spot planes long before
  any human lookout.

Coo!

German soldier

British infantryman

French soldier

'You are not going to get peace with millions of armed men. The chariot of peace cannot advance over a road littered with cannon.' David Lloyd George

CHAPTER THREE

STALEMATE (1915)

On the Western Front stalemate continued. By the summer of 1915, though there were 4 million soldiers in the trenches, there had been little movement in the front lines since the previous winter. The new British commander, General Douglas Haig, did his best to launch a major attack on the German lines at the Battle of Loos in September 1915, but little ground was gained despite the loss of 60,000 troops and three major-generals.

To be fair to the Allied generals, the Germans were happy to stay put, and in 1915, the British and French had neither the men nor the firepower to attack on a broad front. Both sides were also running out of ammunition at a rapid clip. The big guns were like young birds, always hungry for more, especially the high-explosive shells needed to smash the enemy defences. In September 1914, the French commander General Joffre warned that his artillery would run out of ammunition in another 15 days. In Britain, a huge scandal was whipped up by the newspapers in 1915 over the lack of shells, leading to a new government in May.

Soccer skills

In the Battle of Loos, the London Irish Rifles stormed across no man's land to capture the enemy trenches. Sergeant Frank Edwards, the captain of the regimental football team, kicked a football along in front of the advancing troops. The sight of British soldiers coolly passing the ball from one to another would, he thought, give the enemy their biggest shock of the war. Needless to say, the ball got riddled with bullets. You can still see it in the Regimental Museum.

The devil's porridge

In 1915, the British forces began to run out of cordite, the main explosive used to propel shells and bullets forward at great speed. So the British government built four top-secret (yet cavernous) factories near the modern town of Gretna in Scotland, staffed by 20,000 women and 9,000 men. By 1917, 800 tonnes of cordite was being manufactured each week. Because the cordite turned hair yellow and made workers' teeth fall out, it was known as 'the devil's porridge'. Meanwhile, soldiers in the trenches learned a neat trick: chewing on the cordite in their rifle bullets gave them a fever and a few days off duty.

The French army was still licking its wounds after the near disaster of the first months. But change was afoot. The colourful French uniforms were replaced by horizon blue and khaki outfits and the French soldiers were the first to be given steel helmets. They were also bolstered by the steely resolve of General Joffre, nicknamed 'Papa' by his men due to his round, fatherly shape.

The Germans had also learnt a few lessons. After the Battle of Neuve Chapelle in March

1915, when the British almost broke their lines, they realised the importance of a second line of defence. They dug in even deeper, making a real breakthrough for the Allies even harder. In April 1915, during the Second Battle of Ypres, the Germans used a hideous new weapon for the first time – poison gas. The Allies were horrified – how dare they?! But a few months later the British were at it too, spraying chlorine, or 'Red Star' as it was called, at the Germans during the Battle of Loos. It was a disaster. The wind changed direction and blew the gas back towards the British lines. While gas added to the horror, it wasn't going to win any battles.

East or west?

In London, British politicians and generals couldn't decide whether to pile all their forces into the Western Front or attack somewhere else. The French commander General Joffre was unwilling to let a single soldier leave the Western Front, but when the Russians begged the Allies to attack in Eastern Europe, something had to be done.

All together now

Life in the trenches could be overwhelming. But there was nothing like a good sing-song to lift the spirits. During the Christmas Truce of 1914, the Germans had sung Christmas carols, while the following songs were popular with British soldiers. The originals often contained swear words, a reflection of the pain and anger of the troops on the front line.

- Pack up your Troubles in your Old Kit Bag
- Keep the Home Fires Burning
- It's a Long Way to Tipperary
- If You Were the Only Girl in the World
- Oh! It's a Lovely War
- Take Me Back to Dear Old Blighty
- Daisy Bell
- I Wonder Who's Kissing Her Now
- The Rose of No Man's Land
- Lorraine, My Beautiful Alsace Lorraine
- Send Me Away with a Smile
- A Conscientious Objector
- Goodbye-ee
- Are We Downhearted?

You can find the lyrics to some of these songs on page 178.

The plan to open a new front in the Balkans wasn't such a bad idea. The German High Command had nightmares over the prospect of Balkan states such as Bulgaria, Greece and Romania joining the Allies and creating yet another front. And once the Allies defeated Turkey,[1] which had joined the Central Powers the previous year, there was the added bonus of opening up a new sea route to Russia through the Black Sea.[2]

The French and British decided to launch an attack on the Gallipoli peninsula. This long finger of land controlled the Dardanelles Straits, the narrow channel that links the Mediterranean and the Black Sea. The idea was to knock out Turkey quickly, preventing a Turkish attack on Russia while cutting off the German route to the Middle Eastern oil fields.

The plan, backed by Winston Churchill, the First Lord of the Admiralty,[3] was to capture

1. The Ottoman (Turkish) Empire had joined the Central Powers after the British offer of £4 million to join the Allies was trumped by Germany's £5 million.
2. Germany and Austria-Hungary blocked Russia's land routes to Europe; the White Sea in the north and the Sea of Okhotsk in the east were far from the Eastern Front, and icy and treacherous for much of the year.
3. The minister in charge of the British navy.

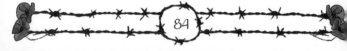

the Dardanelles Straits, then head for Istanbul, the Turkish capital. To keep Joffre happy, Lord Kitchener, the Secretary of State for War, opted for a purely naval attack. This might have worked, but the British admiral in charge, Sir Sackville Hamilton Carden, had a fit of nerves and his second-in-command, Admiral de Robeck, decided to wimp out after three ships were sunk by mines in the Straits. Where was the British stiff upper lip when you needed it?

Kitchener now agreed to a combined land and sea attack, but there was a fatal delay of over six weeks while troops arrived from Britain, giving the Ottoman forces all the time in the world to prepare for the attack. On 25 April 1915, over 50,000 Allied troops steamed toward the beaches on the Gallipoli Peninsula. A third were Australian and New Zealand troops (ANZACs), who landed in the wrong place and were hemmed in by steep hills. At Cape Helles, the sea turned pink with the blood of thousands shot dead before they had even reached the shore.[4]

4. Out of the first 200 soldiers to disembark, only 21 men made it onto the beach.

Toothpicks, toads and jam-pots

Soldiers often gave nicknames to their weapons, probably to make them seem less scary:

- To the French, a bayonet was a 'fork' or a 'toothpick'.

- German field guns were given names like 'Fat Mary', 'Big Bertha' and 'Dear Fritz', while the speedy French 75 mm gun was a 'field hare'.

- The French called their trench mortar the 'toad' because it was short and squat and had a blunt nose, while British Tommies called the German trench gun a 'pipsqueak'.

- The Germans named their machine guns after the sound they made when fired, such as the 'stuttering aunt' or the 'sewing machine'.

- German hand grenades, which had handles, quickly became known as 'potato mashers', while the oval French hand grenades were called 'turtles' by the French and 'Easter eggs' by the Germans.

- Because of the black smoke they made, heavy shells were called 'coal-boxes' by the British and 'jam-pots' by the Germans, while the French called a shell that exploded with a greenish smoke a 'Pernod', after a popular drink.

The Turks suffered heavy casualties too. One Turkish commander, Lieutenant-Colonel Mustafa Kemal,[5] told the 57th Infantry Regiment: 'I do not expect you to attack, I order you to die.' They did, every last man.[6]

The Allies were forced to dig in not far from the beaches. Meanwhile the Turks held the high ground, giving their snipers a great view of the enemy lines. The routine of trench warfare set in. One elderly Turkish soldier was regularly allowed to hang his platoon's washing on the barbed wire without being shot at, while gifts were often flung across no-man's land: dates and sweets from the Ottoman side, and cans of beef and cigarettes from the Allied side.

The Gallipoli campaign continued for ten months, and after another failed landing at Suvla Bay in August 1915, the Allies had little choice but to pull out. Though the evacuation was described in the British papers as a great victory, the Allies had lost 50,000 men for no

5. In 1923, Kemal became the first President of Turkey, after the break-up of the Ottoman Empire.
6. As a sign of respect, there is no 57th Regiment in today's Turkish army.

gain, most from disease,[7] and Lord Kitchener's reputation had suffered a terrible blow. Buoyed by their success, the Turks went on the attack in Mesopotamia and Egypt. Even so, they had lost 87,000 men at Gallipoli, a major blow to their army.

A similar argument over whether to place troops in the east or west was going on in the German High Command. In the blue corner was General Falkenhayn, who said that Germany couldn't win a war fought on two fronts. He wanted to make peace with Russia so Germany could deliver a knock-out blow to France and Britain. In the red corner were Generals Hindenburg and Ludendorff. They wanted to bring Russia to her knees before striking a deal.

In the end, the Kaiser sided with Hindenburg and Ludendorff, partly because Germany had to bail out Austria-Hungary in Galicia. On 13 July, the Central Powers' armies attacked across the entire front, and the Russian line collapsed with the loss of 210,000 men. The

7. *The fierce summer heat led to swarms of flies, which infected wounds and contaminated food supplies.*

Germans pushed on, forcing the Russians into the 'Great Retreat'. By the end of August, most of Poland and Galicia was in Austro-German hands, along with around 750,000 Russian prisoners and a mass of equipment.

As the Russian army retreated, it did its best to destroy anything and everything that might be useful to the enemy. This 'scorched earth' tactic may have slowed down the advancing Germans, but it hurt local Poles a great deal more. The whole of Warsaw was told to leave town, and as the refugees headed east, they brought along deadly diseases such as cholera and typhus. With winter on its way, the German advance was finally halted. But the Russian army, now hundreds of kilometres away from the borders of the Central Powers, was no longer a threat.

The Allied disaster at Gallipoli encouraged Bulgaria to join the Central Powers in September 1915, in a joint attack on Serbia. The previous year Serbia had defeated two attempted Austrian invasions. This time, the Serbs were hopelessly outnumbered and on 9 October Belgrade fell to the Austrians.

Hi-tech death

The Great War saw the introduction of all sorts of terrifying killing machines, as well as big changes in warfare, such as the large-scale use of trains to bring troops to the front (trucks were in their infancy), mobile units with machine guns mounted on motorcycle sidecars, and electric gadgets such as the turrets, searchlights and automatic doors on battleships.

- **Artillery.** This was the real battle winner in the war, especially the very big guns. People could hear the distant thunder of the guns in France as far away as London. The shells were packed with powerful new explosives such as TNT and dynamite. When they exploded, they ripped bodies to shreds, while shrapnel shells burst into thousands of deadly steel fragments that whizzed through the air, killing and maiming even more. Mercifully, many shells were 'duds' that never exploded, while others simply landed in the wrong place. By 1917, British gunners had perfected the 'creeping barrage' that moved ahead of the advancing troops, while pairs of microphones could detect enemy batteries even in dense fog.

- **Light machine guns.** While machine guns dominated the battlefield from the outset, they were heavy and often took a team of men to fire them. The Browning automatic rifle used by American troops in 1918 was the first machine gun that a soldier could fire while walking along.

- **Tanks.** The rumours about the first tanks made them out to be invincible: the stories said they were manned by a crew of 400, as big as a house (with giant guns) and able to outrun a galloping horse. In reality, the first British Mark I tanks were slow, cumbersome and often broke down. They were also incredibly hot and noisy inside and, as they had no springs, crews were thrown about like peas in a can. The French Renault tanks, though lighter, were closer to modern tanks, with a gun in a turret. As for Germany, only about 20 of their giant A7Vs were built.

Mk I tank

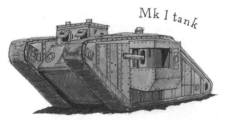

'The Germans ran for their lives –
they couldn't make out what was firing
at them.'

A British infantryman describes the impact of
the first tanks.

- **Air warfare.** At first, rival scouts smiled and waved cheerily at each other. The love didn't last long. Soon they were throwing steel darts, bricks and grenades at each other, or flinging bits of rope to tangle the enemy's propeller. On 5 October 1914, French pilot Louis Quenault opened fire on a German aircraft with a machine gun, and claimed the world's first air-to-air kill. The first air raids were carried out by German Zeppelins, slow-moving airships filled with hydrogen. Later raids were carried out by heavy bombers. Both could bomb targets on the other side of the English Channel. Despite the danger, there were no air-raid sirens in London as it was thought they would cause panic!

Look out below!

The Germans used airships to drop bombs by hand onto enemy cities.

- **Poison gas.** Chlorine gas was released from canisters, then drifted across to the enemy trenches. The gas burned the victims' skin, choking and blinding them. The worst sufferers, usually those lying on the ground, drowned as fluids bubbled up from their poisoned lungs. In short, it was an incredibly painful way to die. When the gas was first used, quick-thinking Canadian troops protected themselves by peeing into pieces of cloth then putting them over their faces. By 6 July 1915, the entire British army was equipped with 'smoke helmets' and other countries soon followed suit. Mustard gas was introduced in 1917. Though not as deadly as chlorine, it could stay in the soil for weeks or even months, blistering the victims' skin, damaging their lungs, and making them throw up.

- **Submarines.** They were used in large numbers for the first time during the Great War. Though self-propelled torpedoes had been around since the 1905 Russo-Japanese war, most German U-boats came to the surface then sank their targets with their gun.

British 'E' Class submarine

With the Bulgarians blocking their retreat south, the Serbs turned west and fled over the mountains to Albania.[8] It was a grim crossing in the middle of winter and over 90,000 troops and civilians died from cold and hunger. Not long after, the German Kaiser and King Ferdinand of Bulgaria congratulated themselves with a big party at Nish (in Serbia) on 18 January 1916. It had been a good year for them. The Russians had been thrown back and the Serbs were well and truly beaten. Now the Germans were free to concentrate on the Western Front, where they would launch their first big attack since 1914.

Italy had watched and waited from the sidelines during 1914. Eventually it joined the side that made the best offer, the Allies, who promised to reward Italy with a big slice of coastline on the other side of the Adriatic Sea. The Italians wasted no time in attacking Austria. But this meant crossing the Alps! Modern war was gruelling enough without the extra hassle of hauling heavy guns and

8. *Some 140,000 Serb soldiers were evacuated by the Allied fleet and taken to the Greek island of Corfu. Here the Serb forces regrouped and later joined Allied troops in northern Greece.*

supplies up sheer cliff faces and glaciers, or having to cope with high altitudes, blizzards and avalanches.[9] It was never going to be easy, and after four battles along the Isonzo river and 300,000 casualties, Italy was back to square one.

Total War

At sea, Britain continued to blockade the German ports, but it was two years before this tactic really began to hurt. Even then, the food shortages and riots in Germany did little to ease the pain of the Allied soldiers in the trenches, as German troops were the last to be affected.

The blockade wasn't bad for everyone. Switzerland, Sweden and especially the United States cashed in as the Central Powers were willing to pay top dollar for goods. To stop vital supplies reaching Germany, Britain used its spy network to find out who bought what from whom, then set up special offices to control the shipping to and from countries such as Holland.[10]

9. In the winter of 1915, 100,000 men died in avalanches alone.
10. It even created a new Ministry of Blockade to run the show.

Kitchener's Mob

- Unlike Germany and France, which had trained reserves of over 4 million men each, Britain only had a small professional army at the beginning of the war. Lord Horatio Kitchener, the Secretary of State for War, launched a wave of propaganda posters, leaflets and newspaper articles designed to create patriotic feelings. In just two months, over 750,000 recruits had volunteered for 'Kitchener's Mob', many joining 'Pals" and 'Chums" battalions in which groups of men from the same village or factory trained and fought with their friends.

- There weren't enough khaki uniforms to go round, so some recruits had to wear the hateful 'Kitchener blue' which made them look like postmen.

- Many old restrictions were ignored. The British and Canadian armies recruited more than 50,000 'bantam-sized' men, below the army's 5 ft 3 in minimum height. They weren't much taller than their own rifles.

- By early 1916, however, the flood of volunteers had become a trickle as people became aware of the grim reality of the Western Front. Britain finally brought in conscription for all men aged 18–41 (though plans to extend this to Ireland in 1918 were met with a wave of strikes and protests).

Germany wasn't going to take the blockade lying down, and stepped up its submarine campaign. Neutral ships were now on the hit list after two U-boats were sunk by HMS *Baralong*, a British warship disguised as a merchant vessel (and sneakily flying an American flag). It was a risky policy. On the morning of 6 May 1915, a luxury passenger liner travelling from the United States, the RMS *Lusitania*, was sunk off the southern coast of Ireland. Almost 1,200 civilians were drowned, including 128 Americans. For a while, the German fleet was forced to withdraw to port, afraid that a continued campaign might bring the United States into the war on the side of the Allies. Up to now, US President Woodrow Wilson had tried to keep the USA out of the war. It was very wise for the Germans to keep it that way.

In the past, most wars had been fought by professional soldiers on distant battlefields. The Great War was the first 'Total War': now millions of ordinary citizens were caught up in the fighting or sent to work in the factories to make armaments. Terrifying modern weapons brought the conflict to people's doorsteps. On

31 May 1915, London was bombed by German Zeppelin airships and over the course of the war, 2,000 British civilians were killed or injured by such raids.

Few countries escaped the fallout of modern war. In Armenia, the invading Turkish forces systematically killed hundreds of thousands of civilians. Russian peasants starved as grain supplies were diverted to the front line, and in Poland millions of civilians caught in war zones were forced to leave their country and shelter in refugee camps. In Serbia, the typhus carried by soldiers heading home on leave killed a third of the population.

The lives of women were affected more than most. Before the war, most thought women shouldn't go to work or be allowed to vote.[11]

11. In Britain, female protestors known as suffragettes campaigned for the right of women to vote. Many were arrested and sent to prison and one, Emily Davison, died in June 1913 after she threw herself underneath King Edward VII's horse during the Derby.

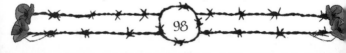

The canaries

By the end of the Great War, nearly 900,000 women worked in factories making shells and bullets. Though munitions jobs were better paid than most, the work was extremely hazardous:

- **Poisoning.** The workers were nicknamed 'canaries' because the explosives, especially TNT, turned hands and faces yellow. One woman complained that her black hair went green, while other workers stole TNT and used it to colour their hair red! Over 60 British workers died of poisoning after chemicals such as TNT got into their bloodstream, while the nasty cocktail of toxic chemicals used in armaments also caused vomiting and depression.

- **Explosions.** Working with explosives was not for the faint-hearted. On 19 January 1917, an explosion at the Silvertown munitions factory in West Ham, London, killed 73 people and injured over 400 others, while an explosion at Nottingham's Chilwell National Shell Filling Factory in 1918 killed 137.

When the first women were trained as doctors in Scotland, there had been riots and Queen Victoria herself complained that it was 'an awful idea'. But the war created new jobs, many for women. They drove buses and trains, operated telephone exchanges and did heavy work in mines, munitions factories and shipyards.

Londoners, Berliners and Parisians tried to go about their business as usual. But it was hard to escape from the war. The newspapers each day listed the dead, missing and wounded, and every family lived in dread of a telegram bearing the opening: *'It is my painful duty to inform you that a report has this day been received from the War Office notifying the death of…'*.

In Britain, anti-German feelings grew as newspapers did their best to stir up hatred. They delighted in reporting enemy atrocities, such as the sinking of the *Lusitania* or the execution of Edith Cavell, a nurse who was shot by a German firing squad on 12 October 1914 after helping British and French soldiers escape to Holland. Another story fibbed that a Canadian soldier had been pinned to a door by German bayonets. This led to a riot in the East

End of London as an angry mob attacked German shops. The government did little to deny such rumours as they gave a big boost to army recruitment.

Not everyone swallowed the lies, though. The thousands who refused to fight were known as conscientious objectors. Often seen as cowards and beaten up in the street, they had to face a tribunal to see if they were genuine[12] or just 'shirkers' who wanted others to do the fighting.

As the conflict dragged into a second year, competing governments braced themselves for a long war of attrition. They took over many industries and changed their machinery to produce weapons and supplies.[13] Total War sounded very impressive, but it cost a fortune and crippled many European countries with debt after the war.[14]

12. In Britain, out of 750,000 cases, some 16,000 men were recorded as conscientious objectors. Around 4,500 of these were sent to do work on farms or in factories, 7,000 worked as stretcher bearers in the front lines, while another 6,000 men were forced to fight, or face prison if they refused.
13. Unfortunately, when the war was over, governments didn't retool the machines back again to make the original products, so many factories went bust.
14. Not surprisingly, the biggest spenders were the ones with the biggest armies and navies: Germany ($37 billion), Britain ($35 billion), France ($25 billion), Russia ($22 billion), and the United States ($22 billion).

Pacifists

- Before the war began, European socialists were heavily opposed to the idea of war, saying that it would lead to workers killing each other in the millions. The French trade unions held mass protests. But once war was declared, most trade unions backed their governments. The French pacifist leader Jean Jaurès was assassinated by a nationalist fanatic on 31 July 1914.

- In Britain, many groups protested against the war, including religious groups such as the Quakers, and the Women's Peace Crusade, which had over 100 branches across the country by the end of the war. Philosopher and pacifist Bertrand Russell was sent to Brixton prison in south London for six months in 1918.

- In the United States, the 'Land of the Free', two new laws made in 1917–1918 gave the government the power to close newspapers and jail anyone who spoke out against the war. When union leader Eugene V. Debs made an anti-war speech in June 1918, he was sentenced to ten years in prison.

DORA

In Britain, the Defence of the Realm Act (DORA), passed in 1914, and the Munitions of War Act of 1915 gave the government enormous powers. The government could take over any land, factory or workshop, and workers were banned from going on strike. DORA also contained a very fussy list of rules that got longer and longer as the war went on:

- No lights after dark.
- No whistling for a taxi after 10 pm.
- No keeping fragments of Zeppelins or bombs as souvenirs (usually ignored).
- No chatting about military matters in public places.
- No hanging around near railway lines or bridges.
- No giving bread to horses or chickens (or ducks in the park for that matter).
- No ringing church bells.
- No buying binoculars for private use.
- No lighting bonfires or fireworks.
- No buying a round of drinks at the pub. (Meanwhile, pub opening hours were cut and beer was watered down).

Most of these rules were relaxed when the war ended. But one change still rules our lives — British summertime. The clocks still go forward in the spring to give more daylight hours in the evening (the original intention was to increase military production).

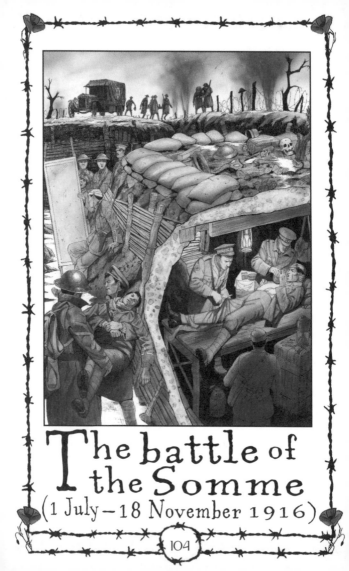

The battle of the Somme
(1 July – 18 November 1916)

CHAPTER FOUR

THE MINCING MACHINE (1916)

The year 1915 had been a complete and utter disaster for the Allies. Joffre boasted he was 'nibbling away' at the Germans, despite the fact that the French had suffered a million and a half casualties. The Germans were equally convinced that they were on top, after a sweeping counter-attack had driven the Russians back in the East the previous year. Yet the best plan Germany's General von Falkenhayn could come up with on the Western Front was to 'bleed France white' and force the Allies to surrender.[1]

---

1. *Or so Falkenhayn said in his memoirs after the war. Some historians think this was a lie to cover up the fact that he had failed to break through at Verdun (see page 106).*

The British commander, Sir Douglas Haig, had other ideas. Rather than grinding down the enemy slowly in a war of attrition, he dreamed of a 'Big Push' towards the English Channel that would knock out the German submarine bases on the Belgian coast. This strategy would cost many tens of thousands of lives — but it was well worth it (in his mind, at any rate). The introduction of conscription in January 1916 would add another 3.5 million soldiers and sailors before the end of the war, giving Haig all the troops (some would say cannon fodder) he needed.

No surrender!

German commander General von Falkenhayn was the first to make a move. He believed the French were on their last legs and that piling on more pressure would make them buckle. In February 1916, the Germans launched a major attack on Verdun, a huge French fortress on the road to Paris. Von Falkenhayn promised the Kaiser that for every dead German soldier there would be three Allied soldiers.

Verdun was a tough nut to crack – and not just because it was the sugared-almond capital of the world (it still is). There were three layers of fortification, all made of concrete and steel. Yet the Germans came very close to a breakthrough, thanks to a blistering 1,200-gun barrage and the equally fiery use of flamethrowers. But Von Falkenhayn didn't reckon on the French, who, inspired by their commander, General Philippe Pétain, were ready to defend Verdun to the last man with the motto 'Ils ne passeront pas' (They shall not pass).

As the months passed, more and more Germans were killed by French artillery, helped by spotter planes from on high. All the while, the French supply lines were kept open by a single road into the city, known as the Voie Sacrée (Sacred Way). By December, the French had clawed back the lost ground, at the cost of 1 million casualties shared between the two sides.[2] No wonder the soldiers likened the slaughter here to a 'mincing machine'.

2. Nine 'lost' villages were also permanently wiped off the map.

Ghosts, angels and ghouls

The carnage of the trenches left many dazed and numb, and exploding shells also created bizarre light effects, so it's hardly surprising that there were many sightings of weird and ghostly things on the battlefield. Back home, many people wanted to believe in stories of angels or miracles, to show that God was on their side.

- At Gallipoli, 800 men were said to have disappeared into a glowing cloud. In fact they had been wiped out by an enemy ambush.

- Many soldiers reported seeing the ghosts of fallen comrades. One myth tells of a Royal Army Medical Corps phantom who emerged out of a poison-gas cloud and began to hand out cups of water, which magically protected drinkers from the gas. Back in England, others reported surprise visits from relatives at the very moment they were killed on the battlefield.

- Perhaps the most famous myth of the war was the Angel of Mons. Several eyewitnesses claimed they saw an angel on a white horse, with a flaming sword, holding back the German advance during the Battle of Mons in 1914. There were also sightings of ghostly castles and horsemen. Such stories probably had their origins in a best-selling book, *The Bowmen*, which was written by journalist Arthur Machen to boost morale.

- The Statue of the Virgin Mary in the town of Albert (near the front line in the Battle of the Somme) was knocked over by a shell but hung on at a crazy angle. The word spread that if the statue crashed to the ground, the fighting would end and the side who started the war would lose.

- Other myths told how pocket-sized copies of the Bible stopped bullets, or claimed that God had put your name and number on the bullet that was going to kill you.

- You may have heard the Great War superstition that if three soldiers lit their cigarettes from the same match, one of the three would be killed. This story was actually invented about a decade after the war by the Swedish match tycoon Ivar Kreuger, to get people to use more matches!

- One story said that bands of wild deserters were living like ghouls in caves under the front lines. Supposedly, they lived by robbing the bodies of dead soldiers. It's easy to imagine how this tale began, given the horrible cries and moans that must have been heard coming from no man's land at night.

In the early summer of 1916, General Joffre urged Haig to relieve the pressure on Verdun, saying that if he waited until August to attack the Germans, the French army 'would cease to exist'. This didn't really suit Haig. He wanted to wait while his new troops were properly trained and the men who were to lead them got more experience in the front lines. But the risk of the French line collapsing was too great.

The big push

Haig's 'Big Push' was to take place near the Somme River. There was no plan other than to throw everything but the kitchen sink at the Germans. For seven days and nights the Allied guns pummelled the German trenches,[3] while 17 giant mines were planted underground,[4] Haig expected this onslaught would wipe out most of the German defenders.

---

3. At the peak of the Somme bombardment, 100 trains a day brought ammunition to the front-line railheads.
4. The first mine to be blown up was caught on film. Buried in a 300-metre long tunnel, 22 metres underground, it took seven months to prepare. The resultant crater was 12 metres deep and 91 metres wide. It's known today as the Hawthorn Crater.

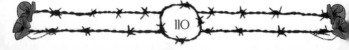

A wave of Allied foot soldiers would then mop up the survivors as the cavalry charged through the gap in the line. It wasn't the worst plan in the world. Unfortunately, the Germans were just 500 metres away and when the big guns kept banging away day after day, they knew something was up. More importantly, their deep trenches and underground bunkers protected them against all but the biggest shells. As soon as the barrage stopped, they hopped back into the front lines and braced themselves for the inevitable attack.

At 7.30 am on 1 July, the bugles and whistles sounded and 11 British divisions – 80,000 men – attacked uphill in a long steady line. The Germans were waiting for them. Their machine guns and shells mowed down wave after wave of British troops, many held up by the sea of barbed wire that the shells had turned into a tangled mess.

By nightfall, the British had suffered 60,000 casualties, their biggest ever loss in a single day. There were few gains that day or in the next few months, despite the first use of tanks

in battle (on 15 July 1916). The Allies battered away at the German lines until late November to keep the pressure off the French forces at Verdun, but an advance of just 9.7 km had cost the lives of over a million men (680,000 Germans and 624,000 Allied troops).

Even if the Tommies had broken through, there was little worth capturing for 50 km. Many of the Pals' battalions were hardest hit, wiping out an entire generation of men in some English villages and towns as well as a large percentage of the men who had joined up from the Canadian island of Newfoundland.

So was it worth it? The Germans had suffered huge casualties too, and their losses in the battles of Verdun and the Somme meant they would probably never win the war on the Western Front. The British army also learned some valuable lessons, albeit at a very high price.

A *living* hell

The war in the trenches was a living hell. Those who weren't blown to tatters, raked by machine-gun fire or maimed by flying shrapnel often went mad or ran away. Some just couldn't come to terms with the fact that they had miraculously survived while all of their friends had died. By the end of the Great War, the British army had suffered 80,000 cases of 'shell shock'. But there was little or no understanding of the trauma suffered by the men in the front lines. In desperation, thousands of soldiers shot themselves in the foot or hacked off a thumb, hoping the wound would get them sent home for good.

Army doctors knew about these tricks. Anyone found guilty of injuring themselves risked being court-martialled and shot by a 12-man firing squad, along with anyone caught deserting or even falling asleep on sentry duty.[5] Smaller offences were punished by Field Punishment No. 1. This meant being

5. *306 British and Commonwealth soldiers were executed during the Great War (including 25 Canadians, 22 Irishmen and 5 New Zealanders).*

strapped to a post for several hours each day, for up to 21 days. Apart from the humiliation, it was terrifying as you couldn't run away if enemy shells started whizzing in your direction.

Many of those executed by the British army were shot for crimes such as desertion and cowardice. In reality, these men were probably suffering from shell shock and just couldn't stand the thought of being on the front line any longer. The story of one British soldier, Arthur Hubbard, gives an idea of what they went through:

Arthur went over the top during the Battle of the Somme in 1916. He was already horrified by the order to kill all prisoners (he shot three Germans who staggered out of a dugout), and then his whole battalion was wiped out by German artillery. Arthur was buried in the mud, and after digging himself out, was almost killed by machine-gun fire as he retreated. He had reached his 'breaking point', and was taken back to a hospital in England to recover from shell shock. In fact, 4 out of 5 men who went to hospital with shell shock were unable to return to the army. But many others were simply given a few weeks' leave then sent back to the front.

Shock tactics

While the Germans were tied up on the Western Front, the Russian fox General Alexei Brusilov made his move against the Austro-Hungarians.[6] Brusilov had been working on a new strategem he called 'shock tactics'. Small units of his very best troops were trained to capture enemy strongholds, some leaping out of secret tunnels dug close to the Austro-Hungarian lines. Helped by short, accurate artillery fire, they punched holes in the enemy lines for the rest of the army to pour through (hopefully with far fewer casualties than usual).

The results were spectacular. Brusilov's attack on 4 June 1916 caught the Austrians completely by surprise. Attacking along a 480-kilometre front, within 10 weeks his forces had advanced up to 96 kilometres. The Austrians and the Germans suffered a staggering 750,000 casualties.

6. This was partly to help out the Italians, as the Austrians had broken through their front line the year before. It worked. Brusilov's crushing victory forced the Austro-Hungarian commander General Conrad to stop his campaign in northern Italy.

Women warriors

During the war, thousands of women served in the armed forces. Although they often worked near the front lines, they rarely fought in battle.

- Between 1914 and 1918 about 80,000 British women worked as auxiliary nurses, ambulance drivers and cooks. They served in France, on the Eastern Front, in Mesopotamia and Gallipoli. Women were only allowed near the front lines in 1915, provided they were over 23.

- One woman managed to see combat with the British army. Dorothy Lawrence, a 20-year-old journalist, disguised herself as a man, helped by two soldiers who cut her hair in the army style. She joined a tunnelling company, but after falling ill she was forced to reveal her true identity. The army was terrified the story would make them look like idiots, so Lawrence was declared a spy and banned from writing about what had happened.

- Another Englishwoman, Flora Sandes, joined the Serbian Red Cross as a nurse. Within 18 months, during the great retreat to Albania, she had exchanged bandages for guns after being separated from her unit. She joined a Serbian regiment where her Serb colleagues affectionately called her 'Our Englishwoman'. Sandes was later injured in combat and was eventually promoted to Sergeant Major. But when she returned to England, she found it very hard to adjust to civilian life and missed the freedom she'd had whilst being treated like a man.

- While Sandes was the only English woman to actually fight, by 1917 the Russian army had a Women's 'Battalion of Death'. This was created after the February Revolution[7] in a last-ditch effort to shame war-weary Russian soldiers to fight. The Battalion of Death was formed by Maria Bochkareva, who with the Tsar's special permission had fought since the beginning of the war. Twice wounded, she was decorated three times for bravery. When the Bolsheviks (a section of the Marxist Russian Social Democratic Labour Party) came to power, she was captured and shot by a firing squad on 16 May 1920.

Poster for Britain's Voluntary Aid Detachments, which provided medical assistance in wartime

7. *The first of two revolutions in Russia in 1917. It was centred around the then capital Petrograd and resulted in the immediate abdication of Tsar Nicholas II and the end of the Russian Empire.*

Romania joined the war on 27 August 1916, hoping to kick the Austrians while they were down and nab Transylvania[8] into the bargain. Why the delay? The Romanian King Ferdinand couldn't make up his mind. He was a cousin of the German Kaiser and had two brothers in the German army – but he was married to a British princess!

Ferdinand should have hung on even longer. The Romanians were soon forced back and by early December 1916 the Central Powers had seized the Romanian capital of Bucharest. The Russian general Brusilov was ordered south to come to the rescue (again), only to lose all the territory he had gained earlier in the year.

The Allies weren't doing much better in the Middle East. In April 1916, the Turks had forced the surrender of the British force inside the city of Kut (in Mesopotamia) after a siege lasting 147 days. At this low point in the British fortunes along came the Arab leader, Sheik Hussein bin Ali. The British persuaded him to help them fight the Turks, promising to

8. A mountainous region that is part of Romania today. It's also famous as the home of the fictional vampire, Count Dracula.

let the Arabs rule themselves once their Ottoman rulers had been defeated.[9]

The resulting Arab revolt was partly inspired by the heroic figure of T. E. Lawrence 'of Arabia'. While British forces under General Allenby attacked the Turkish forces in Palestine, Lawrence cut the Hejaz railway line at the vital moment, creating chaos behind Turkish lines. Boosted by this success, the British captured Baghdad. By the spring of 1917, most of Mesopotamia was in British hands.

On land, it had been a long, brutal year. Needless to say, the Olympic Games, scheduled for Berlin in the summer of 1916, were cancelled.

At sea, the Royal Navy and the German High Seas Fleet finally clashed in the North Sea at Jutland on 31 May 1916. Vice Admiral Reinhard Scheer's speedy squadron pounced on Admiral Beatty's fleet and destroyed two of his battlecruisers. But, thanks again to intercepted radio signals, the British Grand

9. *They lied. The British and French had already secretly agreed to divide up the Middle East between them after the war.*

Fleet under Admiral Jellicoe was soon on its way and caught the German fleet by surprise. Though the British lost more ships and twice as many men in the battle, the main German fleet spent most of the rest of the war in its home ports. This allowed the British fleet to control the seas and tighten its blockade of the German ports.

From the start of the war, both sides were using planes for scouting. By 1915, the first real fighter planes emerged fitted with machine guns. One plane, the German *Eindecker* (monoplane) designed by Anthony Fokker, revolutionised the war in the air. It was fitted with a system that allowed a machine gun to fire straight ahead (without hitting the propeller!). By the winter of 1915, the Allies were losing two to three planes to every Eindecker they shot down.[10]

In 1916, when the first anti-aircraft guns appeared, the Allies worked on better tactics and new planes. The aces of a French squadron, the Storks, showed how to rack up

10. *Things got so bad that the Royal Flying Corps was nicknamed the Suicide Club, while pilots jokingly called themselves 'Fokker fodder'.*

Prince Dynamite

As a student, T. E. Lawrence had learned Arabic in Syria while researching his thesis on the Crusades. After the war broke out, he was posted to the Arab Bureau in Cairo, which sent him to the Hejaz region in Saudi Arabia. Working alongside Emir Feisal, one of Sheikh Hussein's sons, Lawrence was a master of guerrilla tactics. The Arabs called him 'Emir Dynamit' (Prince Dynamite) after he showed them how to blow up bridges and railway lines.

Lawrence also led a remarkable raid on the port of Akaba (in Jordan). He led a small party in a wide arc through the desert before attacking the Turkish defenders from behind. By now, Lawrence was the main link between General Allenby and Feisal's army. He adopted many local customs, such as wearing a long white Arab robe and riding a camel. In the 1920s, Lawrence joined the Royal Air Force under the false name Aircraftman Shaw (possibly to escape attention). His death, in a motorcycle accident in 1935, led to the invention of the motorbike helmet.

Knights of the air

To boost morale, both sides were quick to turn victorious and often glamorous pilots into heroes. Any French pilot who shot down five or more planes became an ace (though German pilots needed 8 and later 16 kills). Here are the top aces by nation:

Manfred von Richthofen (25)* (Germany)
80 kills

René Fonck (59) (France)
75 kills

William Bishop (62) (Canada)
72 kills

Edward Mannock (31) (Britain)
61 kills

Robert Little (22) (Australia)
47 kills

Andrew Beauchamp-Proctor (26) (South Africa)
47 kills

Godwin Brumowski (46) (Austria-Hungary)
35 kills

Eddie Rickenbacker (82) (USA)
26 kills

Numbers in brackets represent age at death.

the kills, but it didn't last long. By 1917, Allied pilots were outclassed by new German planes such as the Albatros and outflown by highly trained German flyers. In just one month, 'Bloody April', 245 British planes were shot down by German pilots. Most famous of all was Manfred Baron von Richthofen, a former cavalry officer who was nicknamed the 'Red Baron' after painting his plane blood-red. Other squadrons began painting their planes a particular (often lurid) colour, so much so that Allied soldiers called them 'Flying Circuses'.

The main targets for fighters were observation balloons. Once you had control of the air, you could stop your enemy from spotting (finding a target) for their big guns. The observation balloons also eliminated the need for spies to go behind enemy lines to see troop formations. In 1915, Captain Ernst A. Lehmann and Baron Gemmingen (Count Ferdinand von Zeppelin's nephew) had come up with the idea of the *Spähkorb*, or spy basket. An observer could be lowered from an airship to navigate and give bombing commands while the airship itself remained above the clouds.

Learning to spy

The Great War saw a huge leap forward in the use of spy tactics such as wire-tapping, code-breaking and intercepting enemy signals.

- The Germans set up several spy schools in German-occupied Antwerp, including one run by Elsbeth 'Tiger Eyes' Schragmüller, who taught her pupils everything from using invisible inks and sketching military installations to codes and ciphers.

- German and Austrian agents carried out more than 50 acts of sabotage against targets in the United States, most famously the Black Tom ammunition dump in Jersey City on 31 July 1916. This was blown up in a giant explosion that destroyed 1,000 tonnes of munitions and had the same effect on the surrounding area as an earthquake.

- The Germans cracked several British diplomatic and naval codes, helping their U-boats to track and sink Allied ships. Meanwhile Room 40, the British code-breaking bureau run by Captain 'Blinker' Hall, got hold of the codes used by German admirals. Sadly, the British top brass never really trusted Hall and didn't make the most of the valuable intelligence he gathered.

- In 1909, the threat from Germany led to the creation of the Secret Service Bureau in

Britain, which soon became MI5 (counter-espionage) and MI6 (overseas spying). MI5 used Girl Guides as messengers in its HQ, as Boy Scouts were too noisy and unreliable.

- Colonel Robert Baden-Powell, who founded the Boy Scouts, would have been very disappointed. A British secret agent, he wandered around the Balkans sketching plans of Austrian fortifications, which were hidden in the wing patterns of the butterflies in his paintings.

- In 1916, Blinker Hall came up with a ruse to make the Germans think there was going to be an Allied landing on the north Belgian coast. The plan backfired when massive German troop movements near the Belgian coast sparked an invasion scare in England.

- In January 1917, a telegram sent by the German Secretary of State, Arthur Zimmermann, was intercepted and deciphered by British code-breakers. It said that Germany would back a Mexican invasion of the United States. When Blinker Hall leaked the telegram to the Americans, together with proof that it was genuine, it was enough to push the United States into the war.

- In the final days of World War I, 14 Choctaw Indian men helped the US army win several key battles by translating radio messages into and out of the Choctaw language. By the end of the war, the German army still hadn't managed to crack the Choctaw 'codes'.

The Red Baron was very superstitious and refused to fly without having been kissed by a loved one.

REVOLUTION! (1917)

By 1917, most countries involved in the war were exhausted after three years of hard slog. Civilians and soldiers alike started to call for an end to the fighting.

It didn't help that the winter of 1916–1917 was bone-chillingly cold. In Paris, the shortage of coal meant that houses were allowed just one electric light on per room.[1] Across the English Channel, horse-racing, county cricket and league football had all been cancelled, while there was a ban on throwing rice at weddings. These were tough times indeed, and to show their support, in July 1917 the British royal

1. *Anyone caught with more than one light on had their electricity switched off for three weeks.*

family changed their name from 'Saxe-Coburg and Gotha' to 'Windsor', to appear less German.[2]

Every country had its problems. Though Britain had promised to allow Ireland to rule itself once the war was over, this wasn't soon enough for some Irish nationalists. On the morning of Easter Monday (24 April 1916), an armed uprising took place in Dublin.[3] After seizing the General Post Office and other buildings, the rebel leader Patrick Pearse proclaimed an Irish republic. Most of the rebels were teachers and workers rather than soldiers. They fought bravely but had no chance against a force of 12,000 British troops armed with artillery and machine guns. After five days of bloodshed in which 450 people died, the uprising was crushed and its leaders were executed. The Irish people were shocked and angry, and public support swung in favour of the rebels.[4]

2. Why did the Royal family wait until 1917? Anti-German feelings were at an all-time high, and it's no coincidence the name changed not long after the three-seater Gotha planes began bombing London in March 1917.
3. The Germans had offered the Irish rebels 20,000 rifles. When the ship carrying the guns was intercepted by the British, its captain sank his own vessel to avoid capture.
4. After a brutal civil war in which over 1,400 people were killed on both sides, Ireland finally won its independence in December 1921.

By early 1917, the French army was completely fed up. Some soldiers even bleated like sheep when their officers walked past – their way of saying that they felt like lambs being led to the slaughter. Things were about to get a whole lot worse.

After the heavy pounding of 1916, the Germans fell back to the Hindenburg Line[5] defences they had been building during the winter. Here they could sit out the heaviest artillery bombardment in the deep caves above the River Aisne. As they retreated, they left behind a wasteland that made any Allied attack through the region impossible for several weeks after.[6] The sudden withdrawal wrong-footed the new French commander Robert Nivelle, who was all set to attack the very positions that now lay empty. Nivelle had bragged that his attack would end the war in 48 hours (he even threatened to resign if it didn't go ahead). He was so confident that his troops were weighed down by three day's worth of rations, while some French tanks carried so much petrol they caught fire.

5. *Known to the Germans as the Siegfried Line.*
6. *In an operation named after Alberich, a spiteful dwarf from Viking mythology.*

Pox in the trenches

The damp conditions in the trenches were a perfect breeding ground for nasty (and often deadly) bugs:

- **Trench foot** was the result of long periods standing in wet, soggy boots. It made the skin go numb and turn red or blue. If untreated the sores turned to gangrene and the foot would have to be amputated. It could be prevented by changing socks and washing feet regularly, but that was easier said than done in the water-soaked trenches.

- **Trench fever** was caused by lice droppings. Though few died from the disease, it was enough to get you taken from the front lines.

- **Typhus** killed millions of German and Russian troops on the Eastern Front. It was also spread by lice that hopped from one soldier to the next as they huddled together in cold weather (fires were banned on the front lines as they gave snipers an easy target).

- **Trench mouth**, caused by stress, poor hygiene and smoking, gave soldiers bleeding gums and bad breath.

- **Malta fever** was caused by eating infected milk or meat and led to fevers, headaches and depression. In the 1940s it was one of the first nasties developed as a biological weapon by the United States, though some US scientists worried it wasn't deadly enough.

- Of the 213,000 British casualties on Gallipoli, 145,000 were due to sickness. The main culprits were dysentery, diarrhoea and pneumonia.

Cutaway view of a British ambulance train in northern France in 1918

You probably won't be surprised to hear that Nivelle's big attack resulted in huge casualties (though they were not all his fault, as his battle plans had been leaked to the Germans). Little territory was won and over 100,000 French troops were killed or wounded. The failed offensive was the final straw for many French soldiers. Some 40,000 troops mutinied, refusing to return to the line. Most simply wanted better food, more leave, and no more crazy attacks on the German line.

For three months, the British were left to hold the line. Remarkably, the Germans did not take advantage, perhaps because they were dealing with mutinies of their own. General Philippe Pétain, the saviour of Verdun, was called in to sort out the mess.[7] Though some mutineers were shot,[8] the stories of whole battalions being wiped out by their own artillery are probably untrue. Pétain also promised better conditions and no more attacks until July. His stick-and-carrot approach worked, and most of the mutineers agreed to go back to the front line.

7. Nivelle had been sacked in May 1917.
8. Just 43 of the 629 mutineers condemned to death were actually executed.

New treatments

One of the few good things to come from the war was a range of new medical treatments:

- Hygiene was taken seriously and antiseptics were used to prevent gangrene in gunshot wounds.

- Casualties were sorted according to how serious their wounds were, the system of triage that is still used in hospitals today (watch any hospital drama and you'll probably hear the word 'triage' mentioned several times).

- Over 40,000 men in the British army alone lost one limb or more. New hospitals were set up to fit them with artificial limbs, but the numbers were so overwhelming it took several years before every victim could be dealt with.

- Surgeon Harold Gillies was appalled by the number of facial wounds he saw in France, many caused by the flying shrapnel from exploding shells. Back in England, he persuaded the army to establish the Queen's Hospital, Sidcup, which specialised in dealing with these wounds. Even so, most victims remained horribly scarred for life.

Goodbye Russia

Big German gains in the east also tipped the balance in Russia. For generations, Russian peasants had been pushed around by the Tsar and in 1905 protests by factory workers in St Petersburg (the Russian capital) had led to a wave of strikes and riots. The war only added to their woes. By 1917, many Russians were on the verge of starvation as food was sent off to the front lines to feed the troops.

As the Russian commander-in-chief, the Tsar was personally blamed for the defeats and the misery of his soldiers. Widespread strikes in the Russian capital[9] in March 1917 were supported by the very troops sent to crush them. Tsar Nicholas II abdicated soon after, but the new government didn't learn from his mistakes. When another attack by Brusilov failed in July 1917, the Russian army had little left to give.

9. *Temporarily renamed Petrograd as St Petersburg sounded too German.*

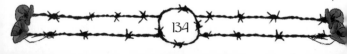

In November 1917, Bolshevik rebels stormed the Winter Palace, the government building, and two days later Vladimir Lenin was declared the new leader of Russia. The Bolsheviks wasted no time in shooting the Tsar and his family and taking Russia out of the war.

Tsar Nicholas II and his family

An armistice was declared in December 1917 and a Russo-German peace treaty was signed at Brest-Litovsk, Russia, on 3 March 1918. The terms of the treaty showed Britain and France what they could expect if they lost the war: Russia was forced to hand over half its industry, most of its coal and iron, and 2.5 million square kilometres of territory, home to a third of its population.[10]

10. Anger at the treaty led to a civil war that lasted for nearly three years.

Winnie the mascot

Most regiments chose mascots that showed how tough or determined they were, such as goats or bulldogs. As he crossed Canada on his way to Europe, Lieutenant Harry Colebourn bought a black bear cub, which he nicknamed 'Winnipeg' after his home town. So far so good. But when his brigade was sent to France, he gave the bear as a present to London Zoo. 'Winnipeg' became a popular attraction, especially with children such as Christopher Robin, the son of author A. A. Milne. When Milne wrote a story about his son and his teddy bear (named 'Winnie' after 'Winnipeg'), the transformation from tough mascot into the cuddly Winnie-the-Pooh was complete.

In northern Italy, Austria and Italy slugged it out along the Isonzo River. But with Russia no longer a threat, the Germans were able to pitch in and the Italians were thrashed at the Battle of Caporetto, losing 700,000 men, mostly prisoners or deserters. Here too, there was a real whiff of revolution. Forty people were killed in anti-war riots in Turin, many led by women furious at the loss of their menfolk.

Even the German war machine was creaking badly under the pressure. A failed harvest in 1916 added to the shortages caused by the Allied blockade. The Germans did their best to paper over the cracks. When flour ran short, bread was made from potatoes. Coffee, known to boost morale, was made from bark, and by the end of the war some 800 alternatives had been created to satisfy the German love of sausages (just don't ask what was in them).

Though not yet starving, most Germans were certainly hungry and city folk went on so-called 'hamster' trips into the country to bribe farmers into selling them food. More and more food was sold on the black market, and if you couldn't pay up, you didn't eat. In return, the German U-boat campaign came close to starving Britain out of the war.[11]

11. *Despite a shortage of torpedoes, German submarines sank nearly 350,000 tonnes of shipping a month in the winter of 1916–1917.*

Hello America!

US president Woodrow Wilson was furious at the German U-boat attacks on civilian ships carrying US passengers (see page 97). When British codebreakers revealed German plans to back a Mexican invasion of the United States, America declared war. It was a major turning point in the conflict.

General Ludendorff had banked on the assumption that the United States would not be able to put a big army into battle before 1919. He was wrong. Though the US army in 1917 was just 100,000 strong, before the end of the war it had sent 2 million men to Europe, with another 2 million in reserve.

It wasn't just about manpower, though. The cost of the war was bankrupting Britain, but now it could be kept afloat by American loans and spending. The news that the Americans were coming was a big boost to propaganda. Leaflets with the news were attached to balloons designed to drift over the German lines.

Though US troops were on their way, General Haig gambled on another big attack in Flanders, combined with an amphibious attack on the U-boat bases in Belgium. He was convinced that the Germans were on the verge of collapse.

For the third time in the war, the British attacked at Ypres, on 31 July 1917. New artillery tactics and even mustard gas were used in the hope of making that ever-elusive breakthrough. The attack started well, capturing the Messines ridge after massive mines erupted under the German lines at 3 am, sending giant mountains of mud into the air.

Then the rains came down, turning the battlefield into a giant mudbath. Slimy shells had to be wiped clean before every shot. Wounded men lying in shell holes slowly drowned, while advancing soldiers, pack animals and equipment simply vanished into the mud and were never seen again.[12]

12. Tens of thousands of bodies are still buried in the mud near the village of Passchendaele.

Lions *led* by donkeys?

This phrase has often been used to describe the British army during the Great War. It suggests that tens of thousands of brave Tommies (the lions) were sent to the slaughter by heartless, incompetent generals (the donkeys). It is sometimes claimed that the phrase was coined by a German general. Its real power comes from the work of writers and war poets like Wilfred Owen, Robert Graves and Siegfried Sassoon, who makes the point very clearly in his poem 'The General':

> *'Good morning, good morning!' the*
>   *General said,*
> *When we met him last week on the way*
>   *to the line.*
> *Now the soldiers he smiled at are most*
>   *of 'em dead,*
> *And we're cursing his staff for*
>   *incompetent swine.*

Various myths have also added fuel to the fire:

Myth 1: British troops were weighed down by their equipment, which made them sitting ducks.
Reality: In 1918 these troops advanced 135 kilometres in 116 days wearing the same gear.

Myth 2: The generals swigged wine in châteaux far behind the lines, while their men were turned into cannon fodder.

Reality: As mobile radios didn't exist, generals had to be near the front line to lead effectively.[13] As a result, 78 British generals were killed in action and another 146 were wounded (compared to 71 German and 55 French generals).

Myth 3: The generals were slow to come up with new tactics.
Reality: This was the first war fought with trenches, barbed wire and machine guns. It was always going to take a while to develop new tactics (the creeping barrage) and new technology (tanks) that would break the deadlock. That said, there's no doubt many British officers were slow to catch on. Before the war, the British High Command felt that having two machine guns made things too difficult for the attackers, and was 'unsporting'.

Myth 4: 'Butcher Haig' had little sympathy for his men.
Reality: It is telling that Haig signed the death warrants for many front-line soldiers suffering from shell shock. But he was no worse than many other generals of the time. Politicians such as British prime minister Lloyd George should also bear some of the blame for not putting a stop to the slaughter.

13. *During the Battle of Cambrai in 1917, the British commander Brigadier-General Hugh Elles led the attack inside one of the leading tanks. When his tank got stuck in a ditch, he was forced to walk back to HQ and command the rest of the battle by telephone.*

By November the Allied attack had ground to a halt, while it was business as usual at the Belgian U-boat bases. Undaunted by the loss of over a quarter of a million men, Haig attacked at Cambrai, the first time tanks were used in large numbers.[14] Though they had a big impact, the Germans counter-attacked and quickly cancelled out any Allied gains. Afraid of a revolt among the troops, the British set up the Ministry of Information in 1918 to keep a close eye on potential troublemakers – but the mutiny never happened.

Though the Allies were still struggling to break through on the Western Front, things were going rather better outside Europe. Making good use of his Australian cavalry, British general Edmund Allenby had captured both Baghdad and Jerusalem. By October 1918, when Allenby seized Aleppo in Syria, close to the border with Turkey, the Ottoman Empire finally agreed to an armistice.[15]

14. 179 out of 378 tanks were lost on the first day, many falling into ditches or breaking down.
15. The Turks had also suffered badly, losing some 2.5 million men (three times the British losses), while their economy had collapsed under the strain of the war: the price of bread went up 50 times after famine hit Syria in 1915.

The Arab revolt continued, with different groups joining and leaving the main Arab force as it headed north. In October, after the city of Damascus was captured, the Arabs set up their own government. Just two days later, General Allenby arrived and coolly announced that Syria was now going to be run by the French. Though the British had promised Arab leaders self-rule, a secret pact with France divided the region up between the two countries. Lawrence (of Arabia) was outraged, but there was little he could do.

This was a war in which there were many losers and few winners. Two empires had already fallen – Russia and Turkey – and Germany, Austria, France and Britain were all hanging on by their fingernails. Though the Americans were on their way, the Russian Revolution allowed Germany to switch troops to the Western Front. It also meant that Britain and France had a new enemy in the east, Communist Russia.

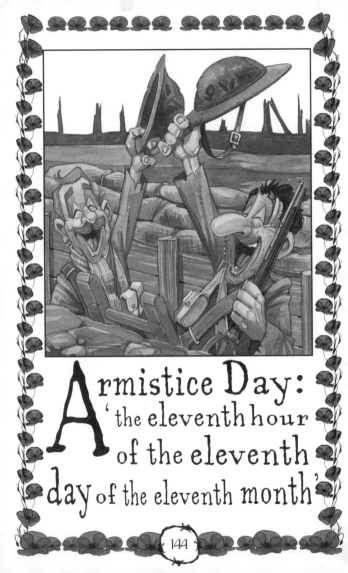

Armistice Day:
'the eleventh hour of the eleventh day of the eleventh month'

CHAPTER SIX

VICTORY AT LAST

Four years on, both sides were still stuck in the mud. With American troops about to arrive in large numbers, it might have made sense for Germany to broker a peace deal, especially given the huge gains they had made in the treaty with Russia (and not long after, Romania).[1]

Instead, General Ludendorff, the joint head of the German army, gambled on one last attack to knock Britain out of the war. Not only did he have a million combat-ready troops fresh

1. *Germany forced Romania to sign the Treaty of Bucharest on 7 May 1918, giving Germany control of her oil for 99 years, control of the Romanian railways and the Danube river, and a monopoly on Romanian trade.*

from the Eastern Front; by the autumn of 1917, the Germans had developed a new way of fighting using their best soldiers – the 'princes of the trenches'.

German stormtrooper

Back in 1915, Captain Willy Rohr had come up with the idea of storm troops, units of tough, mobile soldiers armed with their own machine guns, flamethrowers and mortars.[2] Trained to look for gaps in the enemy line, the storm troops had already shown their worth during the Battle of Cambrai. Attacks were preceded by a short but intense artillery barrage, a tactic masterminded by Georg 'Breakthrough' Bruchmüller.

2. The stormtroopers weren't supermen, but they were well trained, fighting mock battles in dummy trenches behind the lines. They were also quicker than most troops, as they only carried essential kit such as weapons, water and ammunition, and crossed no man's land in small squads of 7–10 men rather than in waves.

Prisoners of war

When the Great War ended, roughly 8 million men were still held in prisoner-of-war (POW) camps. Huge numbers of men often surrendered together: at the Battle of Tannenberg in 1914 over 90,000 Russian soldiers laid down their arms. Though POWs did live longer than troops who weren't captured (they weren't being shot at), they weren't always treated or fed well:

- Germany held about 2.4 million men in around 300 camps. The prisoners slept in hangars or tents, where they dug holes to keep warm. The German guards often beat, starved and bullied the POWs.

- Russia held 2.9 million men, a quarter of whom died from starvation or diseases such as smallpox and typhus.

- Of the 11,800 British soldiers captured by the Turks after the siege of Kut in Mesopotamia, some 4,250 died in captivity, many from starvation.

- Britain and France held about 720,000 POWs, most captured in the last 100 days. While Allied prisoners were sent home at the end of the war, many German and Austrian POWs were forced to work for the Allies until 1920, two years after the war had finished.

If only...

In 1918, British Private Henry Tandey, who later won the Victoria Cross for bravery, had a clear shot of a German soldier struggling to get back to his lines. Instead of pulling the trigger, he let him go. As he explained later: *'I took aim but couldn't shoot a wounded man, so I let him go.'*

According to legend, that German soldier was none other than Adolf Hitler, who saw Tandey lower his rifle. Around 20 years later, the German dictator hung a picture of his 'saviour' on the wall of his mountain retreat at Berchtesgaden.

The German offensive opened on 21 March 1917 with yet another punishing bombardment by the artillery's 'Devil's Orchestra',[3] followed up by a mass attack along a wide front. By a stroke of luck, the stormtroopers were hidden by thick fog until they had almost reached the Allied lines, where they pounced on the enemy with flamethrowers, grenades and machine guns.

3. *A phrase sometimes used to describe the sound of gunfire.*

Ludendorff's gamble had almost paid off. The British were struggling to hold the line.[4] Haig implored his heroes to make one last stand. They clung on, just, while the German advance was slowed down by the lack of artillery support and supplies.

You could argue that the British blockade won the battle. Back home, Germany was starving. In February, millions took to the streets in protest.[5] German troops on the front line were famished too, so much so that they stopped in the middle of the attack to wolf down captured food and drink (including a shipment of Scotch whisky). No wonder then that the attack fizzled out before it reached the vital Allied railhead at Amiens. That said, Britain's food reserves were also running low. It's bacon (literally!) was saved by rationing and the convoy system, in which merchant ships sailed in packs escorted by a navy ship to scare off German U-boats.

4. So many troops had been lost in 1916–1917 that the ranks were now filled by teenagers and 40- to 50-year-olds.
5. Some 400,000 workers went on strike in Berlin alone. The ringleaders were rounded up and executed, and 50,000 workers were put in uniform and packed off to the Western Front.

The forgotten soldiers

British Army

- **Chinese.** China declared war on Germany in 1917 and sent 140,000 labourers to the Western Front. They dug trenches and worked in Allied dockyards, railway yards and arms factories. Most were volunteers, poor farmers lured to the West by the high pay and contracts that promised they would be kept away from the fighting (a lie). Two thousand Chinese war workers are buried in Belgium and northern France. The Chinese got little back in return – in 1919 the Treaty of Versailles handed the German territories in China over to her rival Japan.

- **Sikhs.** India supplied over a million troops by 1919. Of these, 100,000 were Sikh volunteers. The Germans wrongly believed the Sikhs were Muslims, so they sent one group of captured Sikhs to Turkey to fight alongside their 'fellow' Muslims. Still loyal to Britain, the Sikhs escaped and trekked hundreds of kilometres across Asia to a British army outpost in Afghanistan.

- **West Indies regiment.** Around 20,000 men from the West Indies served with the Allied forces, many in the British West Indies Regiment. Though banned from fighting on the Western Front, it fought against the Turkish army in Palestine and Jordan. Over

1,200 West Indians died in action, and another 2,500 were wounded.

- **Africans.** The British recruited troops from the local peoples of southern Africa, including many miners and farm workers in what are now Zimbabwe, Zambia, Mozambique and Malawi. For two years, they fought well in a tough campaign against German and African forces, led by General von Lettow-Vorbeck.

French Army

- **Senegalese.** More than 210,000 men from Senegal in Africa fought for France, 163,000 of them on the Western Front. While the French press praised the bravery of the *Tirailleurs Sénégalais*, racist German propaganda falsely accused them of carrying out atrocities. Some 30,000 Senegalese troops died in battle.

- **North Africans.** Algerian, Tunisian and Moroccan cavalry soldiers known as *Spahis* fought for France on the Western Front, the Eastern Front and in Palestine. They were also used to police Syria after the break-up of the Ottoman Empire.

US Army

- **African Americans.** Over 400,000 African Americans served in the war. But they were badly treated and most were forced to work as labourers behind the lines. However, the men of the 369th Infantry Regiment, also known as the Harlem Hellfighters, were the first US troops to reach the Western Front. They fought for 191 days, longer than any other US unit. One man from the regiment, Sgt Henry Johnson, became the first American to win the French War Cross, the *Croix de Guerre*, after fighting off a raid by 30 German troops with just one other soldier.

German Army

- **Africans.** Over 11,000 African soldiers, known as *Askaris*, fought for the German Colonial Army in German East Africa (now Tanzania) under General von Lettow-Vorbeck. As the war wore on, they were often equipped with uniforms and weapons captured from the British armies in Africa, including woolly hats badly suited to the heat!

By July, it was clear the Germans had failed to break the Allied lines, despite losing another 800,000 men in the attacks. Their army was horribly stretched and ripe for counter-attack. On 8 August 1918, after four long years of trying, the Allies broke through the German lines. They pushed the Germans back 12 kilometres. It doesn't sound much, but General Ludendorff knew this 'black day' was the beginning of the end for the German army.[6]

What was different? By now the Allied gunners had perfected the 'creeping barrage' that allowed their infantry to move up behind a wall of exploding shells, so there was little time for the Germans to get to their posts before the attackers were upon them. Tanks led the charge, including lighter *Whippet* tanks that did a great job of mopping up machine-gun posts.

Over the next 100 or so days, the British did the hard yards, forcing the Germans back to

6. *Ludendorff went into such a spin his doctor suggested that he sing German folk songs when he woke up in the morning. It didn't stop Ludendorff dreaming up mad schemes in which the Turks (now all but beaten) were going to crush the British in Mesopotamia.*

the Hindenburg Line where they had started the year before. Things turned from bad to worse for the Germans as their shattered troops were decimated by malaria and the deadly flu virus that was now on its way across Europe.[7]

The arrival of millions of US troops[8] under General John 'Black Jack' Pershing was the straw that broke the German camel's back. Though only about 400,000 'Doughboys' took part in the fighting, they made all the difference. They were fit, strong, and full of fighting spirit, as they showed in September 1918 when they stormed the German trenches near Verdun.

The Hindenburg line was finally breached on 26 September 1918 using a mix of heavy artillery and tanks. Though the German soldiers refused to give up, the German commanders Hindenburg and Ludendorff realised the war was lost. Even the Kaiser, by now very much on the sidelines, agreed to peace.

7. By now, Germany had also run out of rubber, so their gas masks were useless too.
8. By September 1918 there were over 3 million US troops in France.

five reasons why the Allies won

1. They shared the work. Put simply, the French provided the army, the British the navy, and Russia created a second front. In contrast, Germany spent half the war coming to the rescue of the Austrians.

2. When things got tough, the US bailed the others out with troops and money. The American entry into the war was also a massive boost to morale.

3. This was a war of machines. In the last year of the war, the Allies built more big guns, more tanks and more planes than the Germans – lots more.[9]

4. The Allies won the battle of the big guns (which did most of the killing).

5. By 1918, they dominated the skies. Dogfights won all the headlines, but bombers increasingly did the real damage by targeting trenches, factories, railways and airfields.

9. By 1918, the Germans were building 2,000 planes a month, compared to the 11,000 planes knocked out by the Allied factories.

The other Central Powers collapsed like a house of cards. The Bulgarians agreed to a peace deal two days after the German retreat from the Hindenburg Line began. Austria-Hungary had been a dead man walking since mass strikes in January brought the country to a standstill. By April, the Austrians wanted peace whether or not the Germans were involved. The Allies refused.

Austria's young emperor Karl I desperately tried to patch things up, but to no avail. Poland, Czechoslovakia and Serbia (soon to become Yugoslavia) all declared their independence. On November 1, the once mighty Austro-Hungarian empire vanished forever when the Hungarians decided to go it alone.

I am an officer with all my body and soul, but I do not see how anyone who sees his dearest relations leaving for the front can love war.

Karl I addressing Empress Zita of Hungary after the outbreak of WWI.

On the same day, German sailors were ordered to attack the British fleet. It was a suicide attack and, not surprisingly, they mutinied. There were riots on the streets and revolution was in the air. Kaiser Wilhelm II abdicated and headed across the border to neutral Holland. At long last, at 11 am on 11 November 1918, an armistice between the Allied forces and Germany was signed and the fighting stopped.

The ex-Kaiser

The first thing Wilhelm said after arriving in Holland was: 'Give me a nice cup of hot, good, real English tea.' Partly to disguise his features, he grew a beard, and he spent much of his time hunting. In the 1930s, he hoped the rise of the Nazis would see him back on the German throne, but Hitler blamed him for Germany's defeat in the Great War. Even so, when the Germans captured Paris in 1940, Wilhelm sent a telegram to Hitler saying, 'Congratulations, you have won using my troops.' Though the Kaiser died in 1941, every year German monarchists still commemorate his death in the Dutch town where he lived.

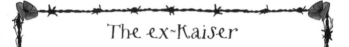

157

The flu virus

- The influenza virus struck without warning. There were stories of people on their way to work suddenly developing the flu and dying within hours. In 1918, children playing in the street skipped over ropes to the rhyme:

  'I had a little bird,
  Its name was Enza.
  I opened the window,
  And in-flu-enza.'

- There was little the doctors of the time could do. Some of the Allies accused the Germans of resorting to biological warfare. Others blamed the illness on the trenches, the use of mustard gas or the 'smoke and fumes' of the war.

- Though the deadly virus probably started in China, it got the name 'Spanish flu' after it killed over 5 million people in Spain in May 1918. Ironically, the fact that large crowds came out to celebrate the end of the war probably helped to spread it even faster.

- The huge numbers of dead were overwhelming. In many countries there were shortages of doctors and nurses, coffins, undertakers and gravediggers.

In the Allied countries, the victory was greeted with great celebrations – and relief. Men and women danced in the streets, paraded and wept with joy that the war was finally over. The partying didn't last long. Just when the worst seemed over, a ferocious flu epidemic engulfed Europe, carrying off millions already weak from the lack of food and the hardship of the war.[10]

Most people wanted to put the hardship of the war behind them. But life was never going to be the same again. Millions of young men were dead – 947,000 of them from the British Empire – and almost every family in Britain, France, Germany and Russia had lost at least one man. Countless thousands of soldiers returned home with crippling injuries or haunted by horrific memories.

Many European countries had massive debts and their economies were badly damaged by the war. In Britain, the soldiers heading home had been promised jobs, but there weren't

10. By May 1919, the Spanish flu, or la grippe, had killed over 200,000 people in Britain and over 27 million others around the world (more people than the infamous Black Death in the Middle Ages).

many to go around. Instead of receiving a heroes' welcome, many ex-soldiers were forced onto the streets to scrape a living. Meanwhile, thousands of women were suddenly expected to give up their jobs for the returning men.

In Germany, the bankrupt government simply printed money to solve its economic problems. This led to financial meltdown. By 1923, German banknotes were worthless – it took a wheelbarrow full of notes to buy a loaf of bread![11] In Russia, three years of civil war ended in a Communist system which led to the death of millions from famine, execution or in Siberian prison camps.

Things did improve gradually, especially in America, where big profits had been made supplying goods to Europe. People wanted to have fun again, and the 'roaring' 1920s were a time of jazz music, dance crazes and trips to the cinema.[12] But in Europe, the hardship of

11. *Economic experts in Britain and France accused the Germans of deliberately destroying their own economy to avoid paying reparations.*
12. *Though the party ended after the Wall St Crash on 29 October 1929, which put millions of people out of work across the world throughout the 1930s.*

the 1920s and 30s led to the extreme politics of the German Nazis and the Italian Fascists.

A permanent peace settlement also had to be arranged, to make sure Europe would never again have to face such a terrible war. US President Woodrow Wilson put forward 14 points that he believed would make a fairer world, including a plan for a League of Nations (a bit like the modern United Nations) that would find a peaceful way to end disputes between rival countries. Wilson's vision of world peace was not shared by the French and British. They wanted revenge on Germany. There were calls of 'Hang the Kaiser' and 'Squeeze Germany until the pips squeak.'

Although the Armistice was agreed in November, it was another six months before the Treaty of Versailles was signed between the Allied powers and Germany, on 28 June 1919 (exactly five years after the assassination of archduke Ferdinand).

Stop fighting!

- Though the Armistice was signed at 5 am on 11 November, the fighting was supposed to end at 11 am so there was plenty of time to let everyone know. Some commanders stopped fighting immediately. Others carried on until the very last minute, and in those final six hours thousands of men on both sides were needlessly killed or wounded.

- At 10.45 am French soldier Augustin Trébuchon died while spreading the news that hot soup was on its way to celebrate the Armistice. But the last man to die in the Great War was US soldier Henry Gunther, at 10.59 am, even though the German soldiers were shouting and waving at his unit to fall back.

- Sixty years after the Armistice was signed, the man who typed it admitted that much of it was back to front. The culprit, Henri Deledicq, had put the carbon papers used to copy the document the wrong way around. Half of the Armistice was unreadable, but luckily it was 5 am so everyone was too tired to notice.

- The rail carriage in which the Armistice was signed and the site on which it stood became a national monument. Almost 22 years later, in June 1940, Hitler made the French surrender in the same carriage.

- The team responsible for putting together the Versailles Treaty completely forgot about the tiny state of Andorra (not hard, given that its army was 11 men strong), so technically it was still fighting the Great War when the Second World War started in 1939! Realising the error, Andorra hastily signed a private peace treaty with Germany so it could become neutral.

- In the United States, the rumour spread that the Armistice was going to be signed on 7 November, four days early. Angry crowds refused to believe the war wasn't yet over and tore up the papers stating the true facts!

- After the Armistice, the German High Seas Fleet was anchored at the British navy base at Scapa Flow in Scotland. Fearing that all of his ships would be seized by the Allies, the German commander, Admiral Ludwig von Reuter, decided to deliberately sink, or 'scuttle', his fleet. Despite British attempts to push sinking ships towards shallow water, 52 out of 74 ships sank in deep water.[13]

13. Many of the wrecks were salvaged over the next few years and towed away for scrapping. The few that remain attract hundreds of scuba divers each year.

The treaty was harsh on the defeated Central Powers. It forced Germany to slash the size of its army and navy and to hand over its overseas colonies, while chunks of Germany were given to Belgium, Poland, France and Denmark. But what angered the Germans most was the war-guilt clause that blamed them for the start of the war, and the resulting reparations (fines) of £6,600,000,000[14] for all the 'loss and damage' suffered by the Allies.

Many German soldiers were bitter. They felt they had not been defeated but 'stabbed in the back' by politicians back home. Such feelings led to widespread support for the aggressive policies of Adolf Hitler in the 1930s.

Though there were mass protests on the streets, there was little the German people could do. An Allied army of occupation, including 200,000 British soldiers, stayed in Germany for another ten years. The cruel effects of the blockade would not be quickly forgotten, and Allied soldiers were shocked by the sight of thin, starving German children.

14. *That's over US$380 billion in today's money. The final reparations payment was only made on 3 October 2010, nearly 92 years after the country's defeat by the Allies.*

The Treaty of Versailles had its heart in the right place. The politicians who drafted it hoped there would be less conflict if smaller peoples were allowed to form their own countries. But the treaty caused as many problems as it solved. The unhappy German giant at the heart of Europe was now surrounded by a patchwork of newly formed and weaker countries such as Poland, Czechoslovakia and Yugoslavia.

The Ottoman Empire was also carved up, with France and Britain grabbing Syria, Jordan and Iraq, while Palestine, also under British control, was earmarked as a Jewish homeland. The Arabs living there were incensed, as Palestine had been promised to them by the Allies for their help in defeating the Turks.[15] As a result, there have been few years of peace in the region since. Turkey was occupied by the Allies until 1923 when Mustafa Kemal (who had fought at Gallipoli) drove them out and declared a Turkish republic.

15. In 1947, it was divided into a country for the Jews (Israel) and a zone for the Arabs (Palestine).

Remembering the war

In the years immediately after the war, Armistice Day (11 November) was a time to meet up with old chums from the front line, to drink and celebrate. Over the years, however, the celebrations have turned into a gloomy reminder of the horrors of war, partly due to the powerful descriptions by poets and other writers who suffered on the Western Front.

- The British army certainly didn't want people to know what was going on at the time. Lord Kitchener ordered the arrest of any press correspondent found in the field. One reporter, Philip Gibbs, was told he would be shot if he returned to France.

- Many of the newspaper reports were pure propaganda. The men in the trenches must have been gobsmacked as they read accounts that swept the horrors they had seen for themselves under the carpet.

- Official war photographers were not supposed to photograph the mountains of dead or the ugly way that soldiers died. Their pictures were destroyed if they were too bleak.

- No soldiers were allowed to own or use cameras at the front. A few ignored the rules and took cameras such as the 'Vest Pocket Kodak' into the trenches.

- Geoffrey Malins (1886–1940) was one of two official British photographers on the Western Front. He also shot a film, *The Battle of the Somme*, which sold 20 million tickets in just six weeks when it was shown in British cinemas in 1916. Though meant to be a propaganda film, it did show the misery of the trenches as well as dead and wounded British and German soldiers.

- Australian Frank Hurley, nicknamed the 'mad photographer', worked very close to the front lines. To make his pictures look more dramatic, he sometimes cut and pasted different images together (decades before computer programs like Photoshop).

- French photographers were among the first to take colour pictures of war, known as *autochromes*, which used microscopic coloured grains of starch.

- During World War I, photographers Arthur S. Mole and John D. Thomas travelled around the United States taking bizarre photos of recruits grouped together to look like patriotic symbols such as the Statue of Liberty, the American Eagle and even President Woodrow Wilson.

Even before the ink on the Treaty of Versailles was dry, the peacemakers had their doubts. The British prime minister David Lloyd George said:

We shall have to do the whole thing again in 25 years' time at three times the cost.

He wasn't far wrong – the Second World War started 20 years later and four times as many people were killed.

The Great War was over, but sadly, it wasn't the 'war to end all wars' that people thought at the time.

famous ex-soldiers

The 20th century would have been very different without these survivors of the First World War. Though they survived, note that many of them were injured in some way.

Film stars

- Humphrey Bogart (1899–1957), later a famous movie star, joined the US Navy in the spring of 1918. Though he spent most of his time ferrying troops back from Europe, according to one story he got the famous scar on his face after his lip was cut by flying shrapnel on the USS *Leviathan* (though others claim a navy prisoner did the damage with his handcuffs).

- Hungarian actor Béla Lugosi (1882–1956) is best known for his portrayal of Count Dracula and other horror villains in the 1930s. During the Great War he fought for the Austro-Hungarian Army from 1914 to 1916. Real name Béla Blaskó, he became a captain in a ski patrol and received his country's highest award for valour after being wounded three times fighting the Russians in the Carpathian mountains.

Artists

- Walt Disney (1901–1966), perhaps the world's best-known cartoonist and cartoon movie maker, dropped out of school in 1917 to join the US army. Rejected because he was still just 16 years old, Disney joined the Red Cross and was sent to France. Though he only arrived after the Armistice was signed on 11 November 1918, Disney spent a year driving an ambulance – which he painted in cartoons!

- French painter Georges Braque (1882–1963), a good friend of Pablo Picasso and co-founder of the Cubist style of painting, served in the French infantry. He was very badly wounded in 1914 and returned to painting in 1917.

- English sculptor Henry Moore (1898–1986) was called up on his 18th birthday and injured by poison gas in 1917 during the Battle of Cambrai. He later recalled that for him, 'The war passed in a romantic haze of trying to be a hero.'

Authors

- Ernest Hemmingway (1899–1961), who became a famous US writer, was rejected for combat in the Great War due to a bad ear from boxing, but served as a Red Cross ambulance driver. He arrived in Paris as the city was being shelled by German artillery, and was later stationed at the Italian Front, where he was wounded and given an award for bravery by the Italian government.

- F. Scott Fitzgerald (1896–1940), the famous US author of *The Great Gatsby*, left university to join the US army but never saw action as the war ended soon after.

- A. A. Milne (1882–1956), author of *Winnie-the-Pooh*, joined the British Army in 1914 and served as an officer in France from 1916, where he wrote comical plays to lift the morale of the soldiers, but he was sent home after becoming seriously ill.

- C. S. Lewis (1898–1963), author of *The Chronicles of Narnia*, was wounded by a British shell that fell short at the Battle of Arras in 1918.

- Lewis's close friend J. R. R. Tolkien (1892–1973), author of the famous *Lord of the Rings* trilogy, fought at the Battle of the Somme but was sent back to England after a nasty case of trench fever. He later wrote that 'By 1918, all but one of my close friends were dead.'

Architect

- Walter Gropius (1883–1969), architect and founder of the famous Bauhaus movement in the 1920s, served as a sergeant major in the German army on the Western Front. He was wounded and almost killed, and earned an Iron Cross for bravery.

Politicians

- After the failure of the Gallipoli campaign, Winston Churchill (1874–1965) resigned as First Lord of the Admiralty and spent some time at the Western Front after becoming a Lieutenant-Colonel in the Royal Scots Fusiliers in 1916. He later became famous as Britain's prime minister during the Second World War.

- Charles de Gaulle (1890–1970), the future French president, was a captain on the Western Front in the French Army. He was wounded several times and made five attempts to escape German prisoner-of-war camps after being captured at Verdun in 1916.

- Adolf Hitler (1889–1945), later leader of the German Nazis and one of the most notorious figures in world history, fought in several battles on the Western Front. Twice decorated for bravery, in 1918 Hitler was temporarily blinded by a mustard-gas attack.

- Benito Mussolini (1883–1945) joined the Italian army and served for about 9 months on the front lines. In 1917, he was released from the army after being badly wounded in an accident involving a mortar bomb.

- Future US president Harry S. Truman (1884–1972) was a US artillery captain who kept his battery firing at the Germans until just minutes before 11 am on Armistice Day.

He later gave the order to drop atomic bombs on Japan at the end of the Second World War.

- There's more: two Canadian prime ministers, one Australian prime minister, one West German president, five Hungarian prime ministers, four Turkish presidents, one East German head of state, three Polish prime ministers, two Romanian prime ministers, two Austrian presidents, one Belgian prime minister, two French presidents, one Finnish president, four British prime ministers, three Italian prime ministers and one South African prime minister were all involved in or fought during the Great War!

Generals

- Many famous Second World War generals also served in the Great War, including Americans General George Marshall, General George Patton, General Douglas MacArthur; British Field Marshall Bernard Montgomery; and German General Erwin Rommel.

...and one Pope

- Angelo Roncalli (1881–1963), later Pope John XXIII, was drafted into the Italian Army as a sergeant. He served on the front line with the medical corps, as a stretcher-bearer and chaplain.

Act *like a soldier*

Over the decades, many movies and TV shows have tried to capture life during the First World War, from dogfights in the skies to camel charges in the Arabian desert. Here are ten of the best:

- **Wings (1927).** The only silent film to win a Best Picture Oscar, this adventure film follows two young US pilots and a nurse from the same small town. It contains some thrilling aerial scenes, including the fiery shooting down of a Zeppelin airship which used real footage. As the film was shot in black and white, chocolate syrup was used for blood!

- **All Quiet on the Western Front (1930).** Seen from the German perspective, this haunting anti-war film follows a group of young German soldiers as they fight in the trenches. Its fight sequences were so realistic they have often been used in documentary films of the war.

- **Sergeant York (1941).** This film starred Gary Cooper (who won an Oscar for the role) as a reluctant hero who does not want to fight but finds himself on the front lines in the final month of the war. When his fellow soldiers are threatened, he uses his sniping skills to save them.

- **Paths of Glory (1957).** When a mad attack by French soldiers ends in slaughter, the generals responsible decide to put the blame on three innocent soldiers, who are accused of cowardice and mutiny. Defending them is Colonel Dax, played by Hollywood legend Kirk Douglas. Though much of the film is set in a courtroom, there is also a very atmospheric night raid into no man's land.

- **The African Queen (1951).** Not really a war film, but it was inspired by the real battle between the gunboats of the Allies and Germany on the lakes of East Africa. First World War veteran Humphrey Bogart won an Oscar for his role in the movie. It was shot in Africa, and the cast and crew had to deal with the real-life problems of dysentery, malaria, contaminated drinking water, dangerous wild animals and poisonous snakes.

- **Lawrence of Arabia (1962).** Based on the life of T. E. Lawrence (who in real life was 9 inches (23 cm) shorter than the actor who played him, Peter O'Toole), this beautiful and dramatic film includes some incredible scenes of Arabian soldiers attacking Turkish forces in the Middle East. Be warned, the film is 227 minutes long!

- **The Blue Max (1966).** George Peppard stars as Bruno Stachel, an ambitious German pilot who will stop at nothing to earn the coveted Blue Max, an award for shooting down twenty enemy aircraft. Though the movie is no classic, the fight scenes in the air give a very good idea of how dangerous and risky real dogfights were.

- **Gallipoli (1981).** Though much of this film tells the story of two Australian sprinters, it's one of the few that depict the futile Allied assault on Gallipoli during the First World War, where thousands of soldiers were stuck on the beaches.

- **Blackadder Goes Forth (1989).** This comedy series set on the Western Front reinforced the idea that British generals lived in luxurious French châteaux while their soldiers were wiped out on the front lines. The main character, Captain Blackadder, spends most of the series doing his best to avoid going 'over the top'. He describes the Great War as 'a war which would be a damn sight simpler if we just stayed in England and shot fifty thousand of our men a week'.

- **War Horse (2011).** Directed by Steven Spielberg, this movie tells the moving story of a young English farmhand named Albert and his horse, Joey. When Joey is sold to become a cavalry horse and heads for the Western Front, Albert joins the army to find him again. The granddaughter of Captain Budgett, one of the World War I veterans who had inspired British author Michael Murpungo to write the original story, acted as an extra in the film.

Laugh like a soldier

It's no surprise that soldiers often turned to humour to help them cope with the horrors of the trenches. Remember that Ypres was pronounced 'Wipers' by British soldiers.

> 'There was a young man from Ypres,
> Who was shot in the rear by some snipers.
> The tunes that he played,
> Through the holes that were made,
> Were the envy of all the bagpipers.'

During the 1920s, a collection of Cockney War Stories was published by the *London Evening News*, 'a remembering and retelling of those war days when laughter sometimes saved men's reason'. Here is a typical tale by an ordinary soldier:

The Outside Fare

During the Third Battle of Ypres a German field gun was trying to hit one of our tanks, the fire being directed no doubt by an observation balloon. On the top of the tank was a Cockney infantryman getting a free ride and seemingly quite unconcerned at Jerry's attempts to score a direct hit on the tank. As the tank was passing our guns a shrapnel shell burst just behind it and above it. We expected to see the Cockney passenger roll off dead. All he did, however, was put his hand to his mouth and shout to those inside the tank: 'Hi, conductor! Any room inside? – It's rainin'!'

A. H. Boughton (B Battery, Honorable Artillery Company)

Sing like a soldier

Here is the first verse and chorus from two famous songs sung by British and Irish soldiers on the Western Front.

Pack up Your Troubles

(Written by George Henry Powell in 1915)

Pack up your troubles in your old kit bag,
And smile, smile, smile!
While you've a Lucifer to light your fag,
Smile, Boys, that's the style.
What's the use of worrying?
It never was worth while.
So, pack up your troubles in your old kit bag,
And smile, smile, smile!

It's a Long Way to Tipperary

(Written by Jack Judge in 1912)

It's a long way to Tipperary,
It's a long way to go.
It's a long way to Tipperary,
To the sweetest girl I know.
Goodbye Piccadilly,
Farewell Leicester Square,
It's a long, long way to Tipperary,
But my heart's right there.

Eat *like a* soldier

ANZAC biscuits

ANZAC biscuits were made by Australian and New Zealand women to send to soldiers fighting in World War One, as the ingredients were relatively easy to get hold of during war time and the biscuits kept fresh for a long time.

Ingredients:

- 2 cups rolled oats
- 1 cup sugar
- 1 cup plain flour
- 1 cup shredded coconut
- ½ cup butter
- 1 level teaspoon baking soda
- 2 tablespoons golden syrup
- 2 tablespoons boiling water

Method:

1. Mix the dry ingredients – the oats, sifted flour, sugar and coconut – in a large bowl.
2. Then melt the butter and golden syrup together, stirring over a gentle heat.
3. After dissolving the baking soda in the boiling water, add it to the melted butter mix.
4. While the mix is foaming, add it to the dry ingredients and stir well.
5. Put teaspoonfuls of mixture on a greased baking tray.
6. Bake for 15–20 minutes at 150°C.
7. Loosen the finished biscuits while still warm, then cool on trays.
8. Eat and enjoy!

Speak like a soldier

Here are some of the slang expressions used by British, Australian and US soldiers in the trenches. Some, like *rookie* and *pukka*, are still in use today:

Archie An anti-aircraft gun.

basket case A person with all four limbs amputated.

battle bowler A steel helmet first introduced in February 1916.

Black Hand Gang A raiding party on a difficult mission.

Blighty England; also, a wound that would get you sent home.

blind pig A mortar bomb.

bonk Artillery shelling.

chats Lice.

chow Rations or food.

coffin nails Cigarettes.

cushy Easy.

daisy cutter A shell designed to explode upon impact with the ground, scattering shrapnel in all directions.

devil dodger An army chaplain.

dixie A British Army camp kettle.

doolally Mad or insane.

Emma Gee A machine gun.

flaming onion A German anti-aircraft shell.

gasbag An airship.

hairy A large British transport horse.

hard tack A soldier's army biscuit.

hedge-hop To fly near the ground.

hop the bags To climb out of the trench and attack.

hush-hush Top secret.

iddy-umpty A signaller.

kick the bucket, go west or **hop it** Die.

Kitch Australian slang for a British soldier (named after Lord Kitchener).

monkey meat French corned beef as described by US soldiers.

Mutt and Jeff The British War and Victory medals.

napoo Australian slang for 'finished'.

old pot and pan A commanding officer.

old sweat An experienced soldier.

pip-squeak A small shell.

pozzy Jam.

pukka Real or good.

pushing up the daisies Dead and buried.

put a sock in it Be quiet!

quick Dick A British gun.

rookie A new recruit.

silent Percy A gun firing so far away it cannot be heard.

sister Susie A woman doing army work.

skilly A very watery stew.

suicide ditch The front-line trench.

Tommy cooker A portable stove.

toot sweet US slang for quick! (from French *tout de suite*).

trench rabbit US slang for a rat.

umpty poo A bit more.

up the jigger In the trenches.

whizz-bang A nearby artillery fire.

woolly bear German shell burst.

yellow cross Mustard gas.

zero hour The time when an attack begins.

Glossary

abdicate To resign from being king or queen.

Allies Russia, France, Britain, Belgium, Italy, the United States and the other countries that fought on their side during the First World War.

ANZAC Australian and New Zealand Army Corps.

armistice An agreement between two sides to stop fighting, so peace talks can take place.

artillery The big guns used in land battles.

assassinate To murder a well-known figure.

Balkans The part of southeastern Europe between Greece and Hungary.

blockade To prevent supplies getting through to enemy ports.

bombardment Continuous heavy shelling by artillery.

casualty A killed or wounded soldier.

cavalry Soldiers that fight on horseback.

Central Powers Germany, Austria-Hungary, Turkey and their allies, such as Bulgaria.

conscription Forcing citizens (especially men aged 18–40) to join the army by law.

convoy A group of merchant ships sailing together, escorted by warships to protect against submarines.

counter-attack An attack by a defending force.

deserter A soldier who leaves his post or unit without permission.

dog-fight One-to-one combat between fighter planes.

draft Another word for conscription.

Eastern Front The war between the Central Powers and Russia.

empire A group of countries under one ruler.

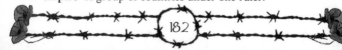

entente An informal agreement to work together.

front Where the fighting takes place.

home front Life for civilians during the war.

kaiser The German word for 'emperor'.

merchant ship A civilian ship that carries cargo or passengers – not a warship.

morale The mood or spirit of people or an army.

munitions Ammunition and equipment used to fight a war, such as shells, bullets, guns and artillery.

mutiny A revolt by soldiers or sailors against their commanding officers, or a refusal to fight.

neutral Not supporting either side in a war.

no man's land The area between the opposing trenches, for example on the Western Front.

offensive An attack or series of attacks.

Ottoman Empire The empire ruled by Turkey.

outflank To go around the side of.

Pals' battalion A group of soldiers all recruited together from the same neighbourhood.

peninsula A piece of land surrounded on three sides by water.

propaganda Books, films and other media that spread ideas, rumours or lies to help one side in a war.

reparations Compensation payments.

shrapnel Fragments of metal from an exploded shell.

treaty A binding agreement between nations.

tsar A Russian word for 'emperor'.

U-boat A German submarine (from the German *Unterseeboot*, 'undersea boat').

Western Front The war between the Allies and the Central Powers in Belgium and France.

Zeppelin A German type of airship.

Timeline of the Great War

1914

28 June Archduke Franz Ferdinand assassinated.

28 July – 4 August Austria-Hungary, Serbia, Germany, Russia, France, Belgium and Britain go to war.

26–30 August Germany defeats Russia at Tannenberg.

4 August – 9 September Von Moltke leads German advance into France. Stopped by generals Joffre (French) and French (British) at Battle of the Marne.

9–14 September Germans defeat Russia at First Battle of Masurian Lakes.

29 October Turkey joins the Central Powers.

30 October – 4 November First Battle of Ypres.

1915

19–20 January First Zeppelin attacks on England.

February Germans begin unrestricted submarine warfare.

25 April – 28 December Allied landings at Gallipoli.

1 May – 18 September German breakthrough at Gorlice-Tarnów forces Russia out of most of Poland.

May Italy joins the Allies. Allied offensive at Artois.

7 May U-boat sinks British liner RMS *Lusitania* with the loss of American lives.

June–December Repeated Italian attacks against Austria-Hungary along River Isonzo.

19 December Haig becomes British commander-in-chief.

1916

21 February Germans begin attack on Verdun.

31 May – 1 June Naval battle of Jutland.

4 June General Brusilov leads Russian offensive.

Timeline

1 July – 18 November Battle of the Somme.

August Romania joins Allies. Hindenburg replaces
  Falkenhayn as German commander-in-chief.

12 December Nivelle is new French commander-in-chief.

1917

January Zimmermann telegram intercepted by British.

February Germans fall back to the Hindenburg Line.

March Nicolas II abdicates after revolution in Russia.
  British capture Baghdad in Mesopotamia.

6 April United States declares war on Germany.

9 April Start of British offensive at Arras.

16 April Failure of Nivelle offensive on River Aisne leads
  to mutiny in French army. Pétain replaces Nivelle.

16 June First US troops arrive in France.

16 July Third Battle of Ypres (Passchendaele) begins.

November Italians badly defeated at Battle of Caporetto.
  Communists take over in Russia, leading to civil war.

9 December British capture Jerusalem.

1918

3 March Germany and Russia sign Treaty of Brest-Litovsk.

April–June Ludendorff offensives on Western Front.

July–August Final German offensive beaten back by
  French counter-attack led by Marshal Foch.

August–October Allied offensives on Western Front.

4 October Germans abandon Hindenburg line.

3 November Austria-Hungary signs armistice.

11 November Armistice on Western Front.

1919

28 June Germany and Allies sign Treaty of Versailles.

Index

Very Peculiar Histories™

Ancient Egypt
Mummy Myth
and Magic
Jim Pipe
ISBN: 978-1-906714-92-5

The Blitz
David Arscott
ISBN: 978-1-907184-18-5

Brighton
David Arscott
ISBN: 978-1-906714-89-5

Castles
Jacqueline Morley
ISBN: 978-1-907184-48-2

Christmas
Fiona Macdonald
ISBN: 978-1-907184-50-5

Global Warming
Ian Graham
ISBN: 978-1-907184-51-2

Golf
David Arscott
ISBN: 978-1-907184-75-8

Great Britons
Ian Graham
ISBN: 978-1-907184-59-8

Ireland
Jim Pipe
ISBN: 978-1-905638-98-7

Kings & Queens
Antony Mason
ISBN: 978-1-906714-77-2

London
Jim Pipe
ISBN: 978-1-907184-26-0

The Olympics
David Arscott
ISBN: 978-1-907184-78-9

Rations
David Arscott
ISBN: 978-1-907184-25-3

Royal Weddings
Fiona Macdonald
ISBN: 978-1-907184-84-0

Other Cherished Library titles

Scotland
Fiona Macdonald
Vol. 1: Ancient times to
Robert the Bruce
ISBN: 978-1-906370-91-6
Vol. 2: Stewarts to
modern Scotland
ISBN: 978-1-906714-79-6

Titanic
Jim Pipe
ISBN: 978-1-907184-87-1

The Tudors
Jim Pipe
ISBN: 978-1-907184-58-1

Vampires
Fiona Macdonald
ISBN: 978-1-907184-39-0

Victorian Servants
Fiona Macdonald
ISBN: 978-1-907184-49-9

Wales
Rupert Matthews
ISBN: 978-1-907184-19-2

Whisky
Fiona Macdonald
ISBN: 978-1-907184-76-5

The World Cup
David Arscott
ISBN: 978-1-907184-38-3

Yorkshire
John Malam
ISBN: 978-1-907184-57-4

Heroes, Gods and Monsters

Heroes, Gods and
Monsters of
**Ancient Greek
Mythology**
Michael Ford
ISBN: 978-1-906370-92-3

Heroes, Gods and
Monsters of
**Celtic
Mythology**
Fiona Macdonald
ISBN: 978-1-905638-97-0

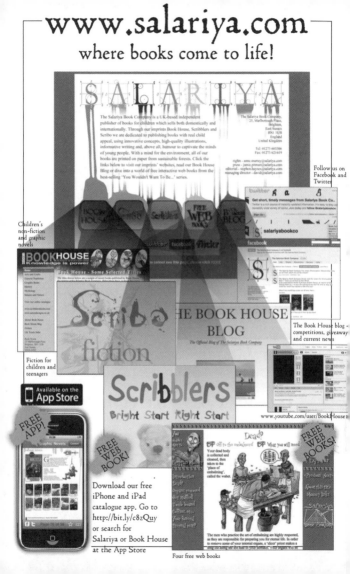

So Jim, he straddled over him
And kept the huns at bay,
And, with both butt and bayonet,
Made wonderful fine play!

He fought like ten big fighting-men.
But huns have no respect.
For valour in an enemy.
They deem it incorrect.

So Jim went down plugged full of holes:
But he was hard to kill.
And, while he lay unconscious, they
Worked out their evil will.

When Jim came to, he found himself
Nailed to a cross of wood.
Just like the Christs you find out here
On every country road.

He wondered dully if he'd died,
And so became a Christ.
"Perhaps," he thought, "All men are
Christs when they are crucified."

His strength was ebbing with his blood.
His hands and feet were dead,
Fierce biting pains shot from the nails.
And blazed within his head.

Below, a mob of jeering huns
Mocked at his woful plight
They bade him loose himself, and come
Down for another fight.

"Christ!" — groaned Jim Baxter,
Through his teeth.
And meant no ill thereby:—
It was his usual expletive
And came most readily.